Fish, Oysters and Shell Fish

"He was a brave man who first ate an oyster."—Dean Swift.

FISH.—With the possible exception of salmon, fish is a less nutritious article of diet than flesh meat, and yet it fitly supplements the latter. The oily and coarser grained species is more nutritious than the white, or finer grained but not so easily digested. A fish is in good condition when its gills are bright clear red, its eyes full and the body firm and stiff. Before cooking they should be well washed in cold water and kept in salt water for a short time, but they should not be allowed to stand in water for any length of time and should be kept upon ice until wanted. Small fish are usually fried or boiled, all large fish to be boiled should be wrapped in a cloth and tied closely with twine, steaming is preferable to boiling. Salmon, bluefish, halibut and shad are very palatable baked in cream. Mackerel is best broiled and should be broiled upon the skin side first; other fish first on the inside. In boiling fish, let simmer gently as hard boiling breaks them; time, eight minutes to a pound, sometimes longer.

BAKED FISH.—Clean and wipe dry a white fish or any good sized fish, stuffing made like that for poultry, but drier. Sew it up and put in a hot pan with drippings and a lump of butter; dredge with flour and lay over the fish a few thin slices of salt pork or bits of butter. Bake half hour, basting occasionally.

BOILED FISH.—All fresh fish, except salmon should be placed in salted cold water for boiling. If placed in boiling water the outside would cook much sooner than the inside. A little vinegar added to the water in which fish is boiled improves the flavor. Put the fish in the kettle with the back bone down, to three or four pounds of fish put a small handful of salt. Boil the fish gently until you can draw out one of the fins easily. Most varieties of fish will be well done in twenty or thirty minutes, some in less time. Serve with drawn butter, with hard boiled eggs sliced, or if preferred, milk sauce.

BAKED WHITE FISH WITH TOMATOES.—Take a white fish or trout that will weigh about three pounds, clean, rub with salt and pepper inside and out. Lay a piece of salt pork, not too fat, in the flesh, put in a covered baking dish and turn over it one pint of stewed seasoned tomatoes, cold tomatoes left over are nice. Bake about forty minutes.

SCALLOPED SALMON.—Place in a baking dish a layer of cracker crumbs, then a layer of salmon, then another layer of cracker and salmon, ending with a layer of cracker. On this pour two cups of milk, one egg whipped. Add salt, pepper and butter size of an egg. Bake.

SALMON CUTLETS.—One cup of hot mashed potatoes and one cup of salmon, mash together and form into cakes, put in a beaten egg, roll in bread crumbs or crackers and fry in hot lard.

FRIED FISH.—Wash the fish thoroughly, wipe dry, sprinkle lightly with salt, dip in beaten egg then roll in cornmeal, fry in hot fat. Note—Above fish recipes were demonstrated in American Cookery series by Mrs. A. McKay.

FISH CROQUETTES.—Two small or one large white fish; boil, bone and chop; add a little salt, red pepper and onions; make gravy of the water the fish is boiled in; add milk, butter and flour; stir in fish, shape into croquette, roll in egg, cracker crumbs and fry in hot lard. Garnish with parsley.

TARTARE DRESSING FOR FISH CROQUETTES.—Take yolk of one raw egg; beat; add a little salt, red pepper, mustard and mix well. Beat in salad oil until thick; let stand on ice until needed. Then add juice of two lemons or half cup of vinegar, one tablespoon of capers, six small cucumber pickles chopped fine and very little onion. Serve cold with hot croquettes.—Mrs. Whitehead.

OYSTER COCKTAIL.—Half pint of catsup, twenty-five drops tabasco sauce, one tablespoonful horseradish, one teaspoonful dry mustard, one teaspoonful lemon juice, oysters, pepper and salt to taste. Put four or five oysters in glass and pour one tablespoon of this sauce over them. Fill glass with finely chipped ice, serve at once.—Mrs. Davidson.

OYSTER COCKTAIL.—A small oyster is used, five or six being alloted each person. For six persons mix together three teaspoons each of vinegar, grated horseradish and tomato sauce; six teaspoons of lemon juice and one of Worcestershire sauce. Have the oysters very cold. Put an equal amount of the prepared sauce over the oysters in each glass. The glass should be placed upon a plate. Serve with an oyster fork and small spoon. This is the prevailing way of serving oysters as a first course.—Mrs. R. J. Walker.

OYSTERS a la BECHEMEL.—Melt three tablespoonfuls of butter and blend it with two tablespoonfuls of flour, add one large cupful of thin cream or milk and cook thick. Plump a scant pint of oysters in their own liquor. Season with one teaspoonful of salt, a dash of cayenne, juice of half a lemon and one-half teaspoon of onion juice squeezed from an onion. Add oysters to the cream sauce and cook two minutes. Serve in pattie shells or on toast.—Mrs. Whitehead.

SALMON LOAF.—One pound can salmon, four well beaten eggs, one cup fine cracker crumbs, one tablespoon melted butter, half teaspoon salt. Remove bones from salmon and mince finely. Mix all together with hands, form into loaf and steam one hour. Serve with following sauce: Take liquid from salmon and add two tablespoons sweet milk, little salt, one tablespoon corn starch, boil all together and pour over loaf.—Mrs. Schollander.

SCALLOPED SALMON.—Place in a baking dish a layer of bread crumbs then a layer of salmon, another crumbs and salmon, ending with crumbs. On this pour two cups of milk, one egg (whipped), salt, pepper and butter the size of an egg.—Mrs. Paul Leonhardy.

OYSTER FRITTERS.—Beat yolks of two eggs light, add one half cup milk and one cup of flour sifted with one fourth teaspoon of salt. Beat well and add one half teaspoon of melted butter. Set aside for an hour or so in a cool place. When ready to use beat the whites of eggs stiff and add them. Take a large oyster in a big spoon, dip it into the batter and filling the spoon and drop into smoking hot grease or fry like doughnuts. Serve with tomato catsup or any preferred sauce.

OYSTER SAUTE.—Drain select oysters, heat pan hot and brown butter in it. Just cover the bottom of the pan with large oysters as soon as the butter sizzles and is piping hot. When brown on under side turn and brown well. Season with salt and pepper. Add butter as needed and turn the oysters and butter sauce on to prepared toast points. Heat the dry pan again, add butter and when hot brown more oysters in it. The butter must be hot and only a few oysters should be browned at a time.

OYSTERS AND BACON BAKED.—Butter a roast pan and lay large plump oysters in a layer on the bottom of it. Season to suit taste with salt, pepper and lemon juice and lay three thin slices of bacon over the top. Roast brown in a quick oven. Serve on toast with tomato sauce, if liked, or with cream sauce. A piquant bake is made by mixing finely chopped green apples with the oysters before baking.

PIGS IN BLANKETS.—Wrap each large oyster in a thin strip of bacon and fasten with a tooth pick, bake in a quick oven until bacon is crisp and oysters plump. Sometimes they are broiled over clear coals.

CREOLE OYSTERS.—Bake in ramekins or individual dishes. Put a teaspoon of butter in the bottom of each dish, then six or seven oysters; add one tablespoon of chili sauce and place a strip of bacon on top of each. Place dishes in a baking pan and bake until bacon is crisp.

SAUCE FOR OYSTER COCKTAILS.—Mix three tablespoons of tomato catsup, three tablespoons of vinegar, one tablespoon of Worcestershire sauce, three tablespoons of grated horseradish, juice of one lemon and salt and pepper to season well. Place on ice. Chill the oysters well, wash and drain them, lay six in each serving glass and cover with the prepared sauce. Serve very cold, with salted wafers.—Contributed.

OYSTERS IN CELERY SAUCE.—Clean and cut celery into small pieces and cook until tender in boiling salted water. Rub enough of the soft celery through a colander to make a cupful. In a saucepan melt a tablespoonful of butter and mix smoothly into it a heaping tablespoonful of flour. Add a cupful of hot milk and cook until creamy; add the soft celery and half a pint of oysters, add more salt if needed, one-eighth teaspoon of pepper and a few drops of lemon juice; cook until the oysters curl, when the filling is ready for the ramekins. Serve hot.

DEVILED OYSTERS.—Butter scallop shells and put into each five oysters with their own liquor and sprinkle with a drop of Tobasco, a little tomato catsup and a quarter-salt-spoonful of salt and cover with fine cracker or bread crumbs. Scatter a few bits of butter here and there on the oysters and set the shells in a hot oven. Serve on doily covered plates.

KIPPERED HERRING.—Rinse herring in warm water, dry and put on tin or agate plate in hot oven 15 minutes; then pour over a little melted butter, cover and leave in 5 minutes more. This should be served on small pieces of toast.

FINNAN HADDIE.—Put a piece of butter the size of a walnut in pan and when hot add two cupfuls of finnan haddie picked fine. Add one cupful of cream or milk into which one tablespoonful of flour has been rubbed smooth. Let come to a boil and when cooled a little add a dash of pepper and the well beaten yolk of an egg. Serve on toast.

SCALLOPED OYSTERS.—Roll one pound and a half of crisp crackers fine. Butter a deep baking dish and spread a layer of crackers an inch deep. Spread over them a dozen oysters in their liquor, sprinkle a generous half teaspoon salt and a dash of pepper over them, dot with bits of butter, (about two tablespoons) and pour in half a cupful of milk, then add another layer cracker crumbs, oysters, etc., and proceed until one quart of oysters and one and one half pounds of crackers are used. Cover the top with cracker crumbs, dot generously with butter and pour on the remaining milk and oyster liquor. Use altogether about one and one half pints of milk to this quantity of oysters and crackers. Bake about one hour or until crumbs are well browned and oysters plump.—Mrs. Whitehead.

SAUCE FOR OYSTER PATTIES.—One cupful of solid oysters. Melt two large tablespoons of butter in a stew pan, blend in two heaping tablespoons of flour and rub smooth; add one scant pint of cream or rich milk; stir until smooth and thick. Drain the oysters and add them with one level teaspoon of salt and a good dash of pepper. When the oysters are plump remove to back of range and stir in the beaten yolks of two eggs mixed with a little cream. For canned oysters add one large teaspoon of curry powder before serving. Serve in pattie shells of baked pastry or in timbal cases or on buttered toast.—Mrs. Whitehead.

OYSTER PIE.—Line a baking dish with rich pastry, either pie crust or biscuit crust. Put one quart of oysters in a double boiler with one cup of milk, and two thirds cup of butter and steam until oysters are plump. Slice six hard boiled eggs, mix with one half cupful of cracker crumbs and a cupful of sweet cream; add one full teaspoon of salt and a generous sprinkling of pepper. Mix with the prepared oysters and fill the lined baking dish. Cover with the top crust and bake about twenty minutes in a hot oven or the pastry shell may be baked separately if preferred and filled with the cream. The thickened, creamed oyster patty filling makes a good filling for oyster pie, also it may be served with steamed dumplings or small baking powder biscuits.—Contributed.

FRIED OYSTERS.—Select large, fresh oysters. Drain them and season with salt and pepper. Roll bread crumbs that have been crisped in the oven very fine and then sift them. Dip each oyster in the prepared crumbs and then into beaten egg and again into the crumbs. Heap the crumbs in thick little piles and roll the oysters in them until a nice thick crust is formed over each oyster. Have an iron kettle or skillet filled two inches deep with smoking hot lard, lay the oysters in a nice frying basket, if you have one, and plunge it into the hot grease. Cook until nicely browned. Drain and serve hot with lemon points, tomato catsup or any preferred sauce.—Mrs. Whitehead.

SALMON TIMBALES.—One can salmon, flaked, add the beaten yolks of three eggs, two tablespoons of thick cream, one teaspoon of lemon juice, salt and pepper and lastly cut in the stiffly beaten whites of the eggs. Pour into greased individual molds, set in a pan of hot water and bake about twenty minutes.

BAKED FISH SCALLOPS.—Two cups cold cooked fish. Remove the bones and break fish into small flakes. Mix with a thick cream sauce, well seasoned. Butter baking shells or individual dishes, fill with the creamed fish, cover with fine bread or cracker crumbs, dot with butter and bake until brown. Serve with lemon points.

CODFISH BALLS.—One cup of flaked cod fish soaked in clear water, then drained. Boil three large potatoes until tender, then drain and mash with the cod fish. Season with salt, pepper and butter and add one beaten egg. Drop by the spoonful into smoking hot grease and fry like doughnuts. Serve immediately.

SCALLOPED FISH.—Add flaked cold cooked white fish, halibut or salmon to a thick cream sauce seasoned with minced onions, thyme or parsley and butter, alternate with layers of cracker crumbs and bake brown.

CREAMED FISH CANAPES.—Beat an egg with half a cup of milk and add a dash of salt. Dip circles of bread, cut half an inch thick, in this and fry brown in butter, turning once. Spread with creamed fish or chicken and place a poached egg on top. Dot with butter and sprinkle with salt and pepper and serve for breakfast or lunch.

Game

"Variety is the spice of life."—Cooper.

WILD DUCK ROASTED.—Prepare as for roasting the same as any fowl, parboil for fifteen minutes with an onion in the water to remove the strong flavor. A carrot will answer the same purpose. Stuff with bread crumbs, a minced onion, season with pepper and salt, a little sage and a good supply of butter, roast until tender. Use butter plentifully in basting. One half hour will suffice for young ducks. If bread crumb dressing is not liked, sliced apple stuffed in the duck is very nice.—Mrs. A. McKay.

TO PREPARE VENISON.—Wash clean, dry well with clean dry cloth, salt, pepper and dredge with flour, cut long gashes into roast, place in gashes strips of salt pork or bacon; lay strips on top; place in a bake pan with a very little water, cover roast until nearly done, take off cover, baste and brown slightly.—Mrs. A. McKay.

BROILED PRAIRIE CHICKEN.—After dressing lay on ice for a few hours, then divide in halves, again divide the thick sections of the breast, sprinkle with salt and pepper and lay the pieces on a gridiron the inside down. Broil slowly at first. Serve with cream gravy and currant jelly.

PRAIRIE CHICKEN (STEAMED AND BAKED).—Stuff them with a dressing of bread crumbs and seasoning of pepper and salt, mixed with melted butter, sage, onion or summer savory may be added if liked. Secure the fowl firmly with a needle and twine. Steam until tender, then remove to dripping pan; dredge with flour, pepper and salt, and brown delicately in oven. Baste with melted butter. Garnish with parsley and currant jelly.

Above game recipes given in American Cookery demonstration by Mrs. A. McKay.

BROILED VENISON STEAK.—Venison steaks should be broiled over a clear fire, turning often. It requires more cooking than beef. When sufficiently done season with salt and pepper, pour over two tablespoonfuls of currant jelly, melted with a piece of butter. Serve hot on hot plates. Delicious steaks, corresponding to the shape of mutton chops are cut from the loin.—Mrs. C. C. Mackenroth.

ROAST VENISON.—Rub the saddle or haunch of venison with a damp cloth and then rub in butter. Make a thick paste of flour and water and spread it an inch thick on the roast. Lay a buttered coarse wrapping paper or one of the new cooking paper bags over the roast and put the meat in the roasting pan with one cupful of hot water. Lift the paper and baste every fifteen minutes with melted butter and hot water. Roast in a hot oven until the meat is tender, then remove the paper and the coat of paste. Dredge the meat with flour, one teaspoonful of salt and pepper and baste with pan drippings and butter until meat is nicely browned. Add a pint of hot water to the drippings and thicken with flour for a gravy. Add a pinch of cloves, nutmeg and mace and stir in a glass of currant jelly until it is dissolved. Strain and serve with the meat. Venison cooked this way will be moist instead of dry and hard.—Mrs. Whitehead.

ROAST PRAIRIE CHICKEN.—Have chicken skinned and put in cold water at least three hours, then wipe dry and stuff with bread crumb dressing. Put in roaster and dot with bits of butter and two or three slices of bacon, one onion pricked with three cloves, add several pepper and all spice kernels and a teaspoonful of salt and one cupful of water. Roast about one and one half hours and baste occasionally.—Mrs. J. Bruegger.

ROAST WILD DUCK.—It is best to keep wild ducks a few days after they are killed if the weather is cold. As most wild duck have the flavor of fish, therefore it is advisable to parboil them, with a carrot in each duck, before roasting, as this absorbs all the unpleasant taste. An onion has the same effect, but when onion is used in dressing the carrot is preferable. Roast the same as tame duck and use dressing for stuffing fowl with a little onion added; bake about one half hour in very hot oven, carefully turning them, baste them and add a little water if necessary. A few slices of bacon roasted with it adds to the flavor of wild game. Serve hot with the gravy it yields. The canvas back duck requires no spices or flavors to make it perfect, as the meat partakes of the flavor of the food the birds feed upon, which is wild celery, and this delicious flavor is best preserved when roasted quickly with a hot fire.—Mrs. George Bruegger.

PRAIRIE CHICKEN OR SQUAB PIE.—After the chickens are picked and drawn as a large fowl is for roasting, wash them and put them in a saucepan with a close cover; they should be covered with boiling water and boiled slowly till tender, when a little salt and an onion and cloves should be added; then take them out, drain and dry, and put in each squab a teaspoonful of butter, a little pepper, salt, minced parsley and thyme; then put into the cavity of each chicken a hard boiled egg; lay them in a large baking dish three or four inches deep; strain over them the liquor in which they were simmered, add teaspoonful of butter, one teacup of milk or cream; sift in two tablespoonfuls of cracker crumbs, put in a few slips of parsley, cover with a rich crust and bake.—Contributed.

Poultry

"Take the goods the Gods provide thee."—Dryden.

ROAST TURKEY.—Select if possible a young turkey, carefully remove all feathers and singe it over a burning paper on the stove, then see that it is carefully drawn and no internals broken; remove the crop carefully; after the head is cut off, tie the neck close to the body, by drawing the skin over it, now wash the inside of the turkey in several clean waters, into the next to the last add a teaspoonful of baking soda, this is to destroy that sour taste which fowls often have, if not freshly killed. After a thorough rinsing and washing of the bird wipe dry both in and outside with a clean cloth, rub the inside with salt, then stuff the body and breast with dressing for stuffing fowls, then sew up with strong thread, rub it over with a little soft butter, sprinkle over some salt and pepper, dredge with a little flour, place in a roaster with a little water and cook from two to two and a half hours, turn it around occasionally so that every part will be browned alike, when it appears done, pierce with a fork and when the liquid runs clear, the bird is done. Serve with cranberry sauce. Garnish with parsley, or fried oysters.—Mrs. George Bruegger.

DRESSING FOR STUFFING FOWL.—For an eight or ten pound turkey use about three pints of stale bread crumbs, put into a dish and pour tepid water over it, (not hot for that makes it heavy) let stand for a few minutes, then take up a handful and squeeze dry with both hands, put into another dish and when all is pressed dry toss it up lightly through your fingers, this process makes it very light. Parboil the liver, heart, and gizzard, in a little stew pan. When tender mince very fine and add to the bread, now one teaspoon of salt, a little pepper, half cup of melted butter; peel and chop one cooking apple, two tablespoons of green or dry fine minced parsley; mix well, add one beaten egg, mix again and it is ready for either turkey or chicken. For goose or duck add a few slices of onion chopped fine. The water in which the heart, gizzard and liver were stewed may be used with the gravy of the roast turkey, goose, duck or chicken.—Mrs. George Bruegger.

ROAST GOOSE.—The goose should not be more than eight months old, and the fatter the more tender and juicy the meat. After the goose has been well washed, cleaned and wiped, rub a little salt inside, stuff with the dressing for stuffing fowls with a little onion added to the dressing. Do not stuff too full and stitch the openings firmly to keep the flavor in and the fat out. Place in roaster with a little water and bake about two and a half hours, carefully turning it frequently and baste with water and salt. When done with all parts evenly brown, take up, pour off the fat and to the brown gravy left, add a little water, and some flour to thicken, bring to a boil and serve in a gravy boat. Garnish goose with parsley.—Mrs. George Bruegger.

VIRGINIA FRIED CHICKEN.—Dress and cut up chickens, rub each piece with salt and pepper, then dip it into beaten egg, then into flour and fry brown in deep hot fat or butter and lard mixed, or bacon drippings. Cover the skillet and let chicken cook slowly after it is browned well to be sure it is done. Remove chicken to platter and turn out part of the drippings. Add cooking spoon of flour to remaining drippings and cook a minute, then add milk or cream to make gravy. Season with salt and pepper and just before serving add beaten yolk of one egg mixed with a little milk. Serve with chicken. Garnish chicken platter with slices of cold boiled ham or crisp bacon, and corn dodgers and you will have a typical "Old Dominion" dish. I got above recipe from a Virginia woman.—Mrs. Whitehead.

SMOTHERED CHICKEN.—Split a young chicken down back, season with salt and pepper and put in roaster with one cup hot water. Roast (covered) until tender. As it begins to brown make a paste of two tablespoons each of butter and flour, blended, and spread it over chicken, basting often with pan dipper. Add cupful cream to drippings in pan for gravy. If the chicken is large cut into pieces as for frying before roasting this way.—Mrs. Whitehead.

CREOLE STEWED CHICKEN.—Boil a pint of rice in two quarts of water until half done, then add a cut up fowl with one minced onion, blade of mace, four large mushrooms or half a can, half a chili pepper, teaspoon salt and three or four small tomatoes cut up and one tablespoon butter. Stew gently until chicken is tender, stirring often and adding hot water as needed. Serve in baked pastry shell or on toast. Mrs. Whitehead. Above chicken recipes were demonstrated in Mrs. Whitehead's paper on Southern Cookery.

SWEDISH DUCK FILLING.—One quart of bread crumbs, four good-sized apples, one half cup of browned butter, cinnamon, raisins, and currants to taste. Stuff fowl.—Contributed.

DAIRY LUNCH CHICKEN SANDWICH.—Make a thin batter of one and one half pints of water, one pint of milk, one egg, scant half teaspoon of soda, one tablespoon of salt, dash of pepper and flour enough to mix like pan cake batter. Cut a young chicken into quarters, dip it in the batter and fry brown in deep fat. Serve between slices of bread. Garnish with dill pickles.—Mrs. T. A. McKay.

CHICKEN CROQUETTES.—One cup of the white meat of boiled fowl packed in solid, then chopped fine and mashed till like fine powder. Add one half level teaspoon salt, one half saltspoon paprika, or white pepper. Make one pint thick cream sauce, with two level tablespoons butter and two heaped tablespoons of cornstarch cooked together, diluted with one pint of hot cream, and stirred till very smooth and thick. Season with one half teaspoon salt and one half saltspoon pepper. Stir as much of the hot sauce into the chicken as it will take up and enable you to handle the mixture in shaping, remembering that the sauce will be much thicker when cold, and so the mixture may be quite soft. The meat varies greatly in its power to absorb the sauce, therefore it is impossible to give an exact amount but if the sauce is thick a large portion may be used and the croquettes will be all the more creamy for it. When cold, shape a tablespoon of the mixture into a ball, then into a cylinder, roll in fine dry bread crumbs, beaten egg diluted with water, then crumbs again, and fry one minute in deep, smoking hot fat. More of the delicious flavor of the meat will be retained with this simple seasoning of salt and pepper than with a variety of condiments.—Contributed.

CREAMED STEWED CHICKEN.—Cut up fowl as for fricassee, put over the fire in enough cold water to cover it well. Bring gradually to a boil. When it begins to bubble, add a stalk of celery, some chopped parsley, and a bay leaf. Simmer until tender before seasoning. Make a white sauce in a frying pan of two tablespoons butter cooked with the same quantity of flour. As soon as well mixed stir into this a large cupful of strained and skimmed gravy from the pot, have ready one half cup cream, heated with a pinch of soda, add this to the thickened gravy, very slowly so as not to curdle. Do not boil after cream is in. Cook dumplings in the gravy left, after the reserved cupful and chicken are taken out.

DUMPLINGS FOR CHICKEN STEW.—In a pint of flour, sift a heaping teaspoon baking powder, one fourth teaspoon salt, sift flour twice, now rub in a tablespoonful of shortening, and wet with enough milk to make a dough that can be rolled out. Cut into rounds and drop into the boiling gravy. Should be done in ten minutes.—Mrs. Paul Leonhardy.

CREAMED CHICKEN.—Three pounds of chicken boiled tender in salted water and freed of bones, skin and gristle. Cut the meat into small pieces. Boil two sweet breads tender in salted water with the juice of half a lemon. When tender, drain and throw them into cold water to blanch; then free from skin and gristle and cut into small pieces; drain a can of French mushrooms and cut them into quarters. Make a cream sauce of two tablespoons of butter, melted and blended with two tablespoons of flour, add one pint of hot thin cream, one teaspoon of salt, juice of one lemon, and juice pressed from half a small onion, and a dash of pepper, cook thick but remove from fire and add one beaten egg yolk mixed with one cup of whipped cream. Add to the heated chicken, mushrooms and sweet breads. Mix well and serve in patty shells, or timbales. (The whipped cream may be omitted.) For escalloped chicken turn the above mixture into a buttered baking dish, cover with fine rolled bread crumbs, dot with butter and bake until well browned. Reserve the chicken broth for soup or make a gravy of it and serve with baking powder biscuit or dumplings.—Contributed.

CROQUETTES.—Cook one large tablespoon of butter with two tablespoons of flour, add one cup milk or cream, one teaspoon onion juice, one teaspoon salt, dash of pepper and nutmeg and one beaten egg. Mix with one cup of minced meat or chicken, form into croquettes after the mixture has stood an hour. Fry brown in deep fat after rolling in egg and bread crumbs.—Contributed.

HOT TAMALES.—Cook a three pound chicken tender in salted water to cover. Chop chicken meat fine and return bones to the kettle. Cut open six large chilli peppers or chillies, wash, cut out seeds and cut into halves. Cover with boiling water and cook until soft and press through a fine sieve. Brown a golden color two medium sized chopped onions in hot butter, add the chilli pulps with half a cup of chicken broth, cover pan and cook slowly fifteen minutes. Put one quart of corn meal into a bowl and pour over it enough hot chicken broth to make a dry paste; work with the hands into a soft but not wet paste. Have broad six inch long corn husks soaked until pliable in warm water. Open these and down the center of each put a wide strip of corn meal paste; mix the chopped chicken with the chilli mixture and spread it on the corn meal paste down the center; roll up the husks, fold in the ends and tie with narrow strips of husks. The corn meal must surround the chicken mixture. Lay the prepared tamales carefully on top of the bones keeping them above the broth. Sprinkle with a teaspoon of salt and cover the kettle and cook steadily one hour, being careful that the broth doesn't boil over the tamales. For the novice, it is easier to steam the tamales over the broth in a flat covered steamer. Serve very hot in the husks. Minced beef may be used instead of chicken and often one cup of chopped tomatoes are added to the chillies before cooking.—Contributed.

CHILE-CON-CARNE.—Cook chillies as in tamale recipe, add to the sieved chillies one pint of thick strained tomato pulp, one minced large onion, one fourth teaspoon salt and cover and simmer fifteen minutes. Cut dark meat from a boiled or roasted chicken, into small pieces or use small pieces of cooked veal, cover with the chilli sauce and stew slowly one hour or stand over hot water and steam about an hour or until chicken has practically absorbed the sauce.—Contributed.

CHILLI MINO PAN CAKES.—Make a light fritter or pan cake batter and fry cakes in hot olive oil or butter shaking them until they are set. Spread these cakes with chicken and chilli mixture (as prepared for tamales) roll up the pan cakes, pour over more of the sauce, sprinkle with grated cheese and serve immediately.—Contributed.

RICE AND CHICKEN CON-CARNE.—One pint of stewed chicken cut up in chicken broth and seasoned with three cooked chillies (sieved) half a cup of washed rice, half a pint of finely minced cooked tongue, one teaspoon of salt. Stir often and cook until rice has absorbed most of the broth but do not let it scorch. Serve with half a pint of strained tomato cooked with one tablespoon of butter and a little salt.—Contributed.

Meat

> "Room! Make way! Hunger commands. My valour must obey."—Beaumont and Fletcher.

TO JUDGE GOOD BEEF.—Good beef, if young, will be of a bright red color, fine grained and firm to the touch. The fat of a clear straw color with a little of it through the muscles, giving the meat a marbled appearance. The suet should be dry and crumbly and of a darker shade than the fat. In old beef both flesh and fat will be darker, much coarser in fiber and decidedly dry compared with young beef. If the beef is of a pale, dull color, and flabby, it is not well matured; if very dark and colored and coarse grained with deep yellow fat it will be found tough and tasteless and if it bears greenish tints and feels slippery on the surface it is already stale and unfit for use. When meat is tough add a little vinegar or a piece of lemon to the water in which it is boiled. This will result in a shortening of time and a saving of fuel, while the meat will be rendered more easy of digestion; also any slight taint that may be about the meat will be entirely removed by this process. A pinch of baking soda can be used instead of lemon or vinegar.

POT ROAST.—Take a nice piece of the round beef weighing about four pounds, season well with salt and pepper and dust over thoroughly with flour. In a flat bottomed kettle melt a piece of butter the size of an egg, when hot put in the meat, turning until well browned on every side. When roast is brown add a little onion, six cloves, six allspice and enough boiling water to come up half way to the top of the meat. Cook slowly for three hours. When done take out meat, add one tablespoon of flour to a little cold water to thicken gravy.

MEAT BALLS.—Two pounds round steak, put through sausage grinder three times, season with salt and pepper, nutmeg and a little cream. Beat two eggs and mix all together; shape into balls and roll in cracker crumbs and fry in butter to a light brown.

BAKED VEAL CUTLETS.—One and one half pounds of veal cutlets laid in well buttered roasting pan with one cup of water; over this spread dressing made of two cups bread crumbs; two onions chopped fine, two well beaten eggs; butter size of an egg, salt and pepper. Mix well, add water to moisten. Lay tin cover on top of pan to prevent scorching. Bake from half to three quarters of an hour. Remove cover to brown.

ROAST SPARE RIBS.—Trim off ends neatly, crack ribs across the middle, rub with salt, sprinkle with pepper, fold over, stuff with turkey dressing, sew up tightly, place in dripping pan with one pint water, baste often. Turn over once so as to bake both sides equally.

ROAST VEAL LOAF.—Four pounds of veal, one pound of pork, one or two eggs, one cup of crackers rolled fine, one tablespoon of salt, one teaspoon of pepper, one teaspoon of sage, mix and make into roll. Bake three hours.

STEAMED VEAL LOAF.—To two pounds of veal, put through a grinder or chopped very fine, add two teaspoons of salt, one fourth teaspoon pepper, butter size of an egg, one cup freshly grated bread crumbs, two eggs, two tablespoons milk. Knead until well mixed. Butter baking powder cans, coat with bread crumbs and fill compactly with the meat and put on cover. Stand in a kettle of water almost to the top of mold. Boil steadily one and one half hours. When cool take out at once.

STUFFED BEEF STEAK.—Prepare a dressing as for chicken, of one cup of bread crumbs moisten with one tablespoonful of melted butter, one tablespoonful of chopped parsley, salt and pepper to taste. Trim off the fat from a sirloin steak, spread on the dressing; roll up; tie to keep in shape, and bake one hour. Baste often with stock and drippings. When done remove the string that it may not unroll and serve with brown sauce. Mushrooms may be added to the dressing if desired. (Roll may be steamed instead of roasted if desired.)

SAUCE.—Melt and brown one large tablespoonful butter, add to it two tablespoonfuls of flour, stir until it is smooth and brown, then add one pint of the liquid strained from the pan. Stir until it thickens, take from the fire and add one tablespoonful of Worcestershire sauce; season with salt and pepper.

DIRECTIONS FOR BOILING HAM.—Put the ham in cold water over night and boil in the same water in the morning. When done skin it and roll it in crackers mixed with pepper, and put into oven to brown.

VEAL LOAF.—Two pounds of veal chopped, one half pound salt pork, chopped or put through meat grinder twice. Add one egg, twelve crackers, rolled fine, salt and pepper to taste. Bake one and one half hours. (The above meat recipes were demonstrated in American Cookery series by Mrs. A. McKay.)

VEAL STEW, WITH LEMON AND EGG SAUCE.—Four pounds veal, salt and pepper, stew the veal until tender, drain off the broth, leaving barely enough to cover the meat. Beat six eggs and add slowly to them, beating all the time, the juice of three lemons. Pour this over the veal and heat but do not boil.—Mrs. Aaron J. Bessie.

NORWEGIAN MEAT PUDDING.—Take five pounds of round steak, quarter pound beef suet, grind ten or twelve times, add salt, nutmeg, one cup sweet cream, one pint milk, mix well. Bake in pudding tin with funnel in center. Set tin in pan of boiling water. Bake one hour.

PUDDING SAUCE.—Drain liquid from pudding when done. To this add sweet cream, thicken with flour and milk. Season with salt, nutmeg and capers. This will serve ten or twelve people.—Mrs. R. Meidell.

German Cookery

BOILED MEAT BALLS.—One pound of round steak, one egg, one slice of bread, two tablespoons melted butter, one teaspoon salt, a dash of pepper. Trim off all the fat, skin and bones, wash them and put on stove in cold water with one onion, piece of celery, a little parsley and salt to taste. Let boil one hour. Chop or grind the meat, soak the bread in water and press, then mix with all ingredients and form into balls the size of an egg, and boil in the above broth ten minutes. For the gravy brown one tablespoon butter, one of flour, add the broth and stir smooth. Put meat balls into a deep dish and pour gravy over them.—Mrs. J. Bruegger.

MARYLAND BAKED HAM.—Soak a ham over night in cold water and boil it tender in sweet cider or water, putting it on in enough liquid to cover. It must be tender but not broken. Remove the rind, outline the fat on top into diamonds, placing a clove in each. Rub half a cup of maple syrup into ham, sprinkle with pepper, place in oven and brown, sprinkling with sifted bread crumbs if liked. Serve hot or if sliced cold, lay plate and heavy weight on ham over night to make nice firm slices.—Mrs. Whitehead. Southern Cookery demonstration.

LULA'S CORNED BEEF.—Five pounds rump beef or sirloin, five tablespoons salt, three tablespoons brown sugar. Saltpetre size of a hickory nut. Dissolve the ingredients in enough water to cover the beef, and let the meat stand in the brine twenty four hours. Boil meat in the same brine three and a half hours. Quick, simple and good as it gives the purchaser a chance

SALMON SAUCE.—One cup of milk, heated to boiling point and thickened with a tablespoonful of corn starch, the oil from salmons, one large tablespoonful of butter, one egg well beaten, juice of one lemon, cayenne pepper to taste. Add the egg to the thickened milk when you have stirred in the butter and oil. Take from fire, season and let stand in hot water three minutes covered, then put in lemon juice and turn over salmon immediately. Note: Above recipes for sauces were demonstrated by Mrs. A. McKay at Domestic Science club.

HORSERADISH SAUCE.—Add to six tablespoonfuls of grated horseradish the yolk of one egg and half a teaspoonful of salt. Mix thoroughly; add a tablespoonful of good vinegar and then carefully a quarter of a cupful of cream whipped to a stiff froth. If the horseradish is already in vinegar omit the tablespoonful of vinegar and press dry the horseradish. This is one of the nicest sauces to serve with cold mutton or with hot corned beef.

HORSERADISH CREAM SAUCE.—Beat one tablespoonful of cream until stiff. As cream begins to thicken add gradually three-fourths teaspoonful of vinegar. Season with a few grains of salt and a dash of paprika, then fold in one half tablespoonful of grated horseradish root.

SAUCE HOLLANDAISE.—Heat two tablespoons of butter in 2 tablespoons of vinegar and of chopped onion and one half pint of boiling water. Beat the yolks of two eggs light and mix with one tablespoon of flour, one half teaspoon of salt and a saltspoon of pepper. Cook gently in the hot vinegar and water and strain at once into the serving dish. This is nice with fish and with white asparagus boiled, drained and chilled on the ice. Serve the sauce hot.

MUSHROOM SAUCE.—Add one can of mushrooms to white or cream sauce and stand over hot water ten minutes but do not cook. Serve with chicken or sweet bread.

CUCUMBER SAUCE.—Pare four cucumbers, throw them into cold water for half an hour then grate them and drain. Add one tablespoon of grated onion and one half teaspoon of salt, one saltspoon of pepper and two tablespoons of vinegar (Tarragon if convenient). Whip six tablespoons of cream stiff, and stir gradually into the cucumber mixture and serve at once with creamed fish, deviled salt fish or baked or broiled fish or with cold boiled or baked mutton.

CLARET OR WINE SAUCE FOR GAME.—One half pint of claret or sherry, four tablespoons soup stock or water, one tablespoon lemon juice, one teaspoon grated horseradish, one saltspoon paprika and one half teaspoon of salt. Heat gently but do not boil. Serve hot with game.

SAUCE TARTARE.—Add two olives, one pickle or gherkins, one tablespoon of capers and one tablespoon of parsley all chopped fine together, to one half pint of mayonnaise dressing or to hot hallandaise sauce.

MINT SAUCE.—Twelve stalks of fresh mint, one tablespoon of sugar and one half cup of vinegar or lemon juice. Strip the mint leaves from the stalks and wash them, chop them very fine, add the sugar and mix well, add the vinegar, stir well, and cover and stand aside for an hour. Serve in sauce boat, with spring lamb.

APPLE SAUCE.—One pound green apples, one pint water, one half cup sugar. Core the apples but do not pare them. Cook with the water in a covered sauce pan. Press through a colander, add sugar to the pulps and cool. Serve with duck, goose and pork roast.

GOOSEBERRY SAUCE.—One pint green gooseberries, one tablespoon of butter, one saltspoon of grated nutmeg, four tablespoons soup stock, one half teaspoon of salt. Cook the gooseberries tender with the water in a covered saucepan about ten minutes. Press through a sieve and add other ingredients. Rhubarb may be substituted for the gooseberries. Nice with salt meats and mackeral and other salt fish.

CRANBERRY SAUCE.—One quart cranberries cooked with one pint of water for five minutes. Press through a colander, add one pound or two cups of sugar to the hot pulp, stir until melted and then cool. Serve with turkey, chicken, mutton or game and with escalloped oysters.

CURRANT JELLY SAUCE.—Add one glass of currant jelly to four tablespoons of hot water or rich soup stock. Turn this into the dish in which game has been roasted, bring to a boil and serve.

CURRY SAUCE.—One tablespoon butter, cooked with one tablespoon chopped onion, add one teaspoon of curry powder, one tablespoon of flour and stir smooth, then add one half pint of boiling water. Add one half teaspoon of salt and one tablespoonful of lemon juice after the sauce has cooked thick. Serve with canned chicken; with oysters, and with boiled rice, lima beans, cauliflower or cooked tomatoes.

BECHAMEL SAUCE.—Make like cream sauce using half cup of chicken stock and half cup of milk instead of milk alone adding one tablespoon chopped cooked carrots, one tablespoon chopped onion, cooked, and one saltspoon of celery seed. For French Bechamel sauce add one half can mushroom and two tablespoons of cream.

EGG SAUCE.—Add four hard boiled eggs, chopped fine, to cream sauce.

CAPER SAUCE.—Add one tablespoon capers to cream sauce.

BROWN SAUCE.—Drain the liquor from the pan in which meat is roasted reserving about four tablespoons of the fat for the sauce. Leave it in the roasting pan and brown two tablespoons of flour in it over the fire, blending it well. When smooth add one pint of hot stock or water, and a little salt or kitchen bouquet if preferred. To this gravy or meat sauce, variety is given by adding one tablespoon of tomato catsup or of Worcestershire sauce, or of mushroom catsup or of onion juice or one half can of mushrooms.

QUICK TOMATO AND CHILI RELISH FOR LOBSTER, SHELL FISH AND HAM.—Six tomatoes peeled, chopped and drained, two tablespoons minced celery or one half teaspoon celery seed, two tablespoons of vinegar, a little garlic or onion, one chopped chili pepper or one drop of tabasco sauce and one teaspoon of salt. If chili pepper is used bake it until skin cracks open, then peel and seed and chop fine. Let it cool and add to the tomato mixture. This is a relish served when ripe tomatoes are in season. It is not cooked. By substituting one cup of whipped cream for the vinegar and omitting the tabasco sauce, a nice sauce is quickly made to serve with cold beef, mutton or veal.

PIQUANTE SAUCE OR OLIVE OR VINEGAR SAUCE.—One tablespoon of chopped onion, one tablespoon of capers, two tablespoons of chopped pickles, or teaspoon of sugar, one half teaspoon of salt, two tablespoons of vinegar, one half saltspoon of pepper, four tablespoons of soup stock or water, and last if liked, three olives stoned and chopped fine or one tablespoon of minced parsley. Heat the soup stock, add vinegar and other ingredients. Serve with calf's head, boiled mutton, lobster or pigs feet.

SPANISH SAUCE.—One and one half pints stock, one tablespoon gelatine dissolved in water, four tablespoons of butter, two tablespoons of flour, two tablespoons chopped onion, a sprig of parsley, one tablespoon chopped celery, one tablespoon chopped carrot, one bay leaf, three whole cloves, a blade of mace, one teaspoon of salt and half saltspoon of pepper. Boil stock with the seasoning, until it is reduced to a pint, rub flour and butter together and add, cook thick and strain. At the last moment add the gelatine and serve with any fowl or meat that requires a rich brown sauce.

CELERY SAUCE.—One bunch of celery, one tablespoon of flour, and one of butter; one pint of stock, six tablespoons of cream, one level teaspoon of salt, dash of white pepper. Wash and cut up the celery, using green tops. Cook in the stock or water until very tender. Press through sieve; rub flour and butter together and cook in the celery puree, add the seasoning and serve with boiled mutton, chicken or rabbit.

Bread and Rolls

"The loaf is, after all, the thing that's most essential."—J. W. Foley.

WHITE AND RYE BREAD.—While boiling potatoes I save the potato water, about one pint. After it is cooled and only luke warm, I soak in it one cake of yeast foam, one teaspoonful of sugar and a small pinch of ginger, and then let it dissolve until supper time; then take a quart of wheat flour and mix with a little warm water, or water and milk, and add your yeast so that the sponge will not be too thin, but like a stiff batter. Let it stand over night in a warm place to raise. Next morning I divide the sponge, using two thirds of it for wheat bread and one third for rye bread, as you can bake six loaves of bread from one cake of yeast; four of wheat and two of rye. To the two thirds part of sponge I take two quarts of wheat flour, one tablespoonful of salt and water enough to make quite a stiff dough. For the rye bread one quart of rye flour with one and one half cups of wheat flour and one teaspoonful of salt. Knead it same as for wheat bread, then let it raise again and when it has doubled in size, it is ready for the tins and after raising there until light, it is ready for the oven in which if hot it will bake in from three fourths to one hour. Before putting it in the oven, I usually wash it with luke warm milk to give it a nice brown color while baking.—Mrs. John Bruegger. Demonstration of German Cookery, breads and cookies.

GERMAN COFFEE CAKE.—Next comes German coffee cake and rolls. I set the sponge with one cake of yeast as for bread and mix it the next morning with two cups of sugar, one tablespoonful of butter, two tablespoons of lard, three eggs, grated rind and juice of one lemon, a little nutmeg, a teaspoonful of salt, add two quarts of white flour, and knead with milk and water, not quite so stiff as for bread. Let it raise two hours after which put it in tins and let raise again; then melt butter and spread on coffee cake and sprinkle with sugar and cinnamon, and it is ready for the oven and ought to be quickly baked. From this dough you can bake quite a variety, for instance, one dozen rolls, two plain coffee cakes, one dozen raised doughnuts and one loaf cake. For the loaf cake you add one cupful of raisins, a little chopped citron, almond extract, one egg and a little butter, beat well with a spoon and fill in a sponge cake tin and let it raise before putting it in the oven to bake, then bake three quarters of an hour.—Mrs. John Bruegger. German Cookery demonstration.

RYE BREAD.—To one pint of water (luke warm) add one cake of yeast foam, one teaspoon salt, two tablespoons sugar, and one medium sized boiled potato. Mash this fine and mix with the salt and sugar in the water; let this stand until evening, then add enough well sifted flour to make a stiff batter. Set in a warm place to rise over night. Next morning add one quart of luke warm water, one heaping teaspoon salt, one quart of white flour, and two quarts of rye flour all well sifted, and work all together, then knead for ten minutes, adding a little flour from time to time until it ceases to stick to the fingers or mold board, then put into a large bread pan and set in warm place to rise again, until light, then knead again, and make into loaves. Put into well greased bread pans, let raise and bake from one to one and a half hours. When done take out and brush lightly with melted butter or drippings.—Mrs. George Bruegger.

WHITE BREAD.—Scald one pint of milk with three tablespoons of lard then put in bread pan with one quart of warm water; add two tablespoons sugar, two tablespoons salt. Stir in flour to make a thick batter one yeast cake that has been soaked well in water. I make sponge after dinner and let set till evening then mix into a large loaf; let stand till morning. Before breakfast knead into loaves. This will make from three to four loaves of bread.—Mrs. Southard.

GRAHAM BREAD.—Make the yeast sponge as above but add one half cup cooking molasses and a little more sugar. Do not make sponge too thick with white flour. Mix in evening, with graham flour but not quite as stiff as white bread. Graham bread is very slow to raise.

DATE BREAD.—One cup of chopped dates, two cups milk, one third cup sugar, one fourth yeast cake, one fourth cup luke warm water, one half teaspoon salt, five cups of sifted flour. Mix and knead like bread and bake in loaves.

POCKET BOOK ROLLS.—Warm one quart new milk, add one cup butter or lard, four tablespoons sugar and two well beaten eggs. Stir in flour enough to make a moderately stiff sponge. Add a small cup of yeast and set in a warm place to rise, which will take three or four hours, then mix in flour enough to make a soft dough and let rise again. When well risen dissolve a lump of soda, size of a bean, in spoon of milk and work into the dough and roll into sheets one half inch thick. Spread with butter, cut into squares and fold over, pocket book shape. Put in tins, let rise a while and bake.—Mrs. L. L. Lampman.

ROLLS.—Take two teacupsful of light sponge. Add to it one half cup shortening, one cup of sugar and two cups of warm water. Mix with flour and knead but do not make a very stiff dough. Let raise all day. In evening form rolls and let them raise all night. Bake in moderate oven.—Mrs. Harry Hanson.

RAISED BISCUITS.—One cup of flour scalded with generous pint of hot potato water. (Boil potatoes and drain water for this). When cold add one cake of yeast dissolved in luke warm water. Mix this at noon and let it stand, uncovered, until night, then add one pint of warm water and enough flour to make a light sponge, beating well. Let stand until morning in a warm place or in a covered bread pan well wrapped to retain the heat. Add to this sponge in the morning one small cup of sugar, two eggs and one half cupful lard and a generous tablespoon of salt. Mix stiff with flour. Let stand until light then knead well, let raise an hour and knead again and make into biscuits. Put in greased baking pans and let raise until very light. Bake in a moderate oven.—Mrs. George W. Newton.

ALMOND WREATH.—Two ounces of flour; two cakes of yeast; one pint of luke warm milk; a tablespoonful of salt. Mix into a light sponge and let it rise all night. In the morning add six ounces of butter and the same of pulverized sugar, six eggs, one pint of rich cream and enough flour to make a soft dough. Let it rise again until very light. Then roll out with few and swift strokes of the rolling-pin into a sheet less than half an inch thick and cut into strips. Braid these into a coronet about some round object in the center. Or you may make it into a round cake if you like. Shell half a pound of sweet almonds, blanch and shred them and dry in the oven for a few minutes. Then mix them with granulated and coffee sugar and cinnamon and strew over the cakes when you have washed the surface with white of egg to make the mixture stick. Bake in a moderate oven. This quantity will make at least six large cakes.

YEAST.—Three heaping tablespoons flour, two of salt, two tablespoons of sugar. Pour one dipperful of boiling water on this and add twelve mashed potatoes. Add cold water enough to cool for yeast. Add one yeast cake which has been soaked one half hour in tepid water. Use half of this for one baking.—Mrs. A. McKay.

Biscuits, Jems, Pancakes and Fritters

"What an excellent thing did God bestow on man when He gave him a good stomach."—Beaumont and Fletcher.

FRITTERS.—Beat four eggs very light. Do not separate yolks and whites but beat together about five minutes; add one scant cupful of milk, one small teaspoon of salt and just a dash of baking powder (about as large as a small bean). Quickly whisk in enough sifted flour to make a thin pan cake batter. Beat smooth. Drop by spoonfuls into deep smoking hot lard and fry like doughnuts. Drain, and serve immediately with maple syrup, honey or jelly sauce.—Mrs. B. G. Whitehead.

SOUTHERN WAFFLES.—Mix together one scant pint of sifted flour and one generous pint of milk until smooth; add one half cupful of melted butter and the well beaten yolks of three eggs; then the well beaten whites and one half teaspoon of salt. Just before baking add two teaspoonfuls of baking powder and hot lard. Bake in a hot, well greased waffle iron and serve immediately with butter and maple syrup or honey.—Mrs. B. G. Whitehead.

PAN CAKES.—For a family of six, take one quart of butter milk or of slightly clabbered sour milk. Beat into it two level teaspoons of soda and one small teaspoon of salt. Add the beaten yolks of two eggs and then enough flour to make a smooth batter, not too stiff. If too thick add a little more milk. Lastly add one tablespoon of melted butter and the stiffly beaten whites of eggs. Rub the smoking hot griddle with a piece of suet fastened to a skewer or fork, drop butter on by tablespoonful and bake the cakes a nice brown, turning once. Serve immediately on hot plates. These cakes may be served with butter and syrup or they may be spread with jam or jelly and rolled. Using half flour with half corn meal makes good corn cakes or half graham flour for graham cakes.—Mrs. Whitehead.

CORN OYSTERS OR CORN FRITTERS.—Grate eight large ears of corn, or split each row of corn down the center and scrape out all of the pulp. Beat the yolks of two eggs, add them to the corn pulps with half a teaspoon of salt and the beaten whites of eggs and then add enough rolled cracker crumbs to make a thick batter. Fry oyster shape, in deep, smoking fat and put in the oven to crisp while the balance of the cakes are frying. Do not use flour to thicken the batter. The crackers are much nicer and give the true oyster flavor. These are made from fresh, green corn, only.—Mrs. Whitehead.

CORN DODGERS.—Put one cup of corn meal, one half teaspoon of salt in double boiler; add one cup boiling water; beat smooth and add one tablespoon butter. Cook and steam covered for one hour. Butter a griddle, drop by spoonful on it, put down fat and when browned put bit of butter on each, before turning. Good served with broiled ham or cooked in frying pan after bacon or sausage.

HOE CAKE.—Put one quart of white corn meal in a bowl; add one teaspoon salt, add sufficient boiling water to just moisten, stirring all the time, beating to stiff batter. Moisten hands in cold water and make corn meal into small round cakes. Bake on plank in front of open fire three quarters of an hour or fry slowly on griddle. When done pull apart, butter and send to table hot.

BEATEN BISCUIT (VIRGINIA).—Three pints pastry flour mixed with one cup lard; one teaspoon salt, mix together like pie crust. Make into stiff dough with milk or milk and water mixed, and knead well; beat or pound with a rolling pin or mallet one hour. The dough should be smooth and glossy and bits should break off with a snap. Shape in thin, flat cakes. Pick all over with a sharp fork and bake until a delicate brown and until the edges crack a little. Must bake thoroughly or they will be heavy in the middle.

JOHNNY CAKE OR CORN BREAD.—One cup corn meal, one half cup flour, two small teaspoons sugar, two tablespoons butter, or drippings, one beaten egg; salt; one cup of sour milk; one level teaspoonful of soda dissolved in a bit of hot water. Beat well and bake in greased tin. May be made with sweet milk and baking powder if preferred. Makes one pan of bread. The foregoing recipes were demonstrated by Mrs. Whitehead in a paper on Southern Cookery.

POPOVERS.—Cup sweet milk, one egg, two tablespoons melted butter, two cups flour, two heaping teaspoons baking powder. Bake in gem pans in a hot oven.—Mrs. Mary Harvey.

GRAHAM MUFFINS.—One egg, one and one half cups sour milk, one teaspoon soda, a little salt, two tablespoons melted butter, two tablespoons molasses, graham flour to make a light batter. Bake in gem tins.—Mrs. Mary Harvey.

WHEATEN GEMS.—Mix one teaspoon baking powder and a little salt into one pint of flour; add to the beaten yolks of two eggs one teacup sweet milk or cream; a piece of butter (melted) half the size of an egg, the flour with baking powder and salt mixed and the well beaten whites of the two eggs. Beat well and bake immediately in gem pans in a hot oven.—Mrs. L. L. Lampman.

PRUNE BROWN BREAD.—One cup corn meal, two cups graham flour, one half cup molasses, one cup sour milk, one teaspoon soda and same of salt, one cup dried prunes washed, pitted and chopped fine. Scald the corn meal and then add the other ingredients; put in greased tins and steam three hours.—Mrs. L. L. Lampman.

MRS. BURK'S NUT BREAD.—Baking powder. One cup sugar, one egg, two cups sweet milk, a pinch of salt, four teaspoons baking powder, four cups flour, one cup of chopped walnuts or more, mix together, let raise twenty minutes, pour into greased coffee cans (uncovered). Bake in moderate oven till brown (45 minutes or more). Slice cold.—Mrs. S. J. Creaser.

BAKING POWDER BISCUITS.—One quart flour, three teaspoons baking powder, one teaspoon salt, sifted through the flour, mix smooth with three tablespoons of butter and lard in equal portions, mix lightly into a soft dough with about three cups milk. Roll and cut in small biscuits. Bake in greased tins in a quick oven.—Dorothy Whitehead.

SWEDISH TIMBALE CASES.—Beat one egg well; add one fourth cup of milk, a few grains of salt, one teaspoon of olive oil and one half cup of flour or enough to make almost a drop batter. Beat it until very nice and smooth. Pour it into a small cup just large enough to hold the timbale iron. Heat the timbale iron in the hot fat for about ten minutes, then lower it into the batter about one inch, turn it partly over as you take it out so the cases will not slip off, then plunge the iron into the fat and when browned slightly lift it up, and drain and slip the cup from the iron. When all are fried fill the cases with any delicate meat, game, fish or oysters, cut small and warmed in a rich cream sauce.—Contributed.

PANCAKES.—One cup sour milk, half cup of sour cream, small teaspoon soda dissolved in water and stirred in the milk; half teaspoon salt, one teaspoon baking powder mixed with flour enough to make thin batter.—Mrs. L. L. Lampman.

PANCAKES.—Two cups flour, two cups milk, two teaspoonfuls sugar, two teaspoonfuls baking powder, one teaspoonful salt, one tablespoonful melted butter, two eggs beaten separately. Have griddle hot and clean but do not grease. Blueberries stirred into pancake batter, as many as you wish, are excellent.—Mrs. Davidson.

TIMBALES.—One fourth cup flour, one half teaspoon salt, one teaspoon of sugar, one egg (beaten), one tablespoon olive oil or butter. Mix the dry parts together and add milk, egg and olive oil. Strain through sieve. Dip hot tambale iron into the grease then into the batter then into the hot grease to cook. Drain and use as pastry shells for creamed peas, chicken, mushroom or oysters.

WITH BEER.—Timbales are very tender and nice made with stale beer or ale. Let one half pint of beer stand in an open dish over night. Omit the sugar and milk and mix flour with the beer, following other directions as given above.—Contributed.

MRS. ALLEMAN'S APPLE FRITTERS.—One cup flour, one teaspoon baking powder, pinch salt, and yolk of two eggs beaten light, with cup of milk. Grate in three medium sized apples, beat well and fold in stiffly beaten whites of two eggs. Drop by spoonful into hot fat and fry until nicely browned. Drain on brown paper and serve with maple syrup. For corn fritters use one cup of canned corn in place of apples.—Contributed.

POP OVERS.—Two cups flour, two cups sweet milk, two eggs, one teaspoon sugar, one quarter teaspoon salt. Beat well together. Put in hot gem tins and bake in hot oven.—Contributed.

PAN CAKES.—One cup of flour sifted with one teaspoon of baking powder, one half teaspoon of salt and one teaspoon of sugar, add enough milk to wet it, then beat in one egg thoroughly, add three teaspoons of melted butter and then thin to a smooth batter with milk, beat thoroughly and bake on a well greased, hot griddle.—Mrs. A. McKay.

JENNY LIND PANCAKE.—Two eggs, pinch of salt, tablespoonful sugar, small cup of flour, one cup of milk, one half teaspoon baking powder. Bake in an omelette pan, put jelly on top, roll and sprinkle with powdered sugar. —Mrs. Lynch.

DATE MUFFINS.—Beat the yolks of two eggs until light. Add one cupful of milk. Sift together one and a half cupfuls of entire wheat flour, one and a half teaspoonfuls of baking powder and one quarter teaspoon of salt. Add the milk and eggs and a tablespoonful of melted butter, and give the batter a good beating. Now add half a cup of dates chopped coarsely and floured, and last of all add the stiffly beaten whites. Mix. Fill gem pans two thirds full and bake in a moderately hot oven for half an hour. These are excellent.

Sandwiches

"There is no higher art than that which tends toward the improvement of food."—Henry Ward Beecher.

Bread for sandwiches should be at least one day old. Cut into thin slices of uniform size, remove all crust and then cut into the desired shape either with the sharp, pliable knife or a sharp cookie cutter. The butter should be soft enough to spread smoothly and the most essential thing is to have good bread and fresh sweet butter. Meat for filling should either be sliced very thin or chopped fine and other ingredients minced or mashed to make as smooth a paste as possible and mix evenly with the salad dressing or other dressing used. Sandwiches are better eaten as soon as made. If necessary to let them stand an hour or so, wrap the plate of sandwiches in a dampened napkin and put in a cold place so the bread will not become hard and dry. Be careful not to let the dressing run over the outer edge of the slices of bread. Sandwiches must be dainty to be appetizing and easily handled. Cut the slices as thin as you can and make into small triangles or squared sandwiches, or oblong ones two or three inches long.

SANDWICHES.—Mince the white meat of a roast chicken, and mix it with half a can of French mushrooms, chopped fine, and a half cupful of chopped English walnuts. Season to taste with melted butter. Put the mixture between slices of whole wheat bread.

WALNUT SANDWICHES.—Shell English walnuts. Blanch and chop, and to every tablespoonful of nuts allow a good half teaspoonful of cream cheese. Rub well together and spread on thin slices of crustless white or graham bread.

DEVILED EGG SANDWICHES.—Mash the yolks of hard boiled eggs to a powder and moisten with olive oil and a few drops of vinegar. Work to a paste, add salt, pepper and French mustard to taste, with a drop or two of tabasco sauce. Now chop the whites of the eggs as fine as possible or until they are like a coarse powder and mix them with the yolk paste. If more seasoning is necessary, add it before spreading the mixture upon sliced graham bread.

ROAST BEEF SANDWICHES.—Chop rare roast beef very fine, taking care to use only the lean portions of the meat. Sprinkle with salt, pepper and a saltspoonful of horseradish. Mix and make into sandwiches with thinly sliced graham bread.

PEANUT SANDWICHES.—Shell and skin freshly roasted peanuts and roll them to fine crumbs on a pastry board. Add salt to taste and mix the powdered nuts with enough fresh cream cheese to make a paste that can be easily spread on unbuttered bread. Keep in a cold, damp place until wanted.

STUFFED EGGS.—Boil eggs hard and throw them into cold water. When cool remove the shells, cut the eggs in half carefully and extract the yolks. Rub these to a powder with the back of a spoon and add to them pepper and salt to taste, a little melted butter to make the mixture into a smooth paste. If ham is not at hand any other cold meat will do, and either anchovies or anchovy paste may be used. Make the compound into balls about the size and shape of the yolks and restore them to their place between the two cups of the whites.

HAM AND OLIVE SANDWICHES.—Chop lean ham fine and beat into each cupful of the minced meat a tablespoonful of salad oil, a teaspoonful of vinegar, a saltspoonful of French mustard, six olives chopped fine and a teaspoonful of minced parsley. Work all to a paste and spread on thin slices of white bread.

SALMON SANDWICHES.—Small can salmon, one small onion chopped, two hard boiled eggs chopped, and chopped celery to taste. Mix with a good mayonnaise dressing and spread between thin, buttered slices of bread.—Mrs. L. L. Lampman.

HAM SANDWICH.—Run boiled ham through the food chopper or mince it very fine. This may be spread plain on buttered bread or it may be mixed with the ground yolks and whites of hard boiled eggs and mixed with mayonnaise dressing to a paste and spread between thin slices of buttered bread.

ROLLED SANDWICHES.—Cut the crust from a loaf of bread lengthwise of the loaf in thin slices. Butter, spread with the ham mayonnaise paste and roll up like jelly roll, pressing firmly together. Cut in slices like jelly roll cake slices.

NUT BREAD SANDWICHES.—These are made of nut bread slices spread with butter. Raisin bread also makes nice sandwiches and so does date bread.

ENGLISH SANDWICHES.—Spread toasted muffins (cold muffins cut into slices and toasted) with butter, then with cottage cheese or grated cream cheese. Cover with a thin layer of plum (blue damson preferred) marmalade, and cover with top slice of toasted muffin.

SARDINE OR ANCHOVY SANDWICHES.—Mix ground yolks of five hard boiled eggs with three boned sardines or anchovies, mashed, two small pickles or as many capers chopped, one teaspoon of butter. Spread between thin slices of buttered graham bread.

EVENING SANDWICHES.—Three hard boiled eggs, one half pint olives and one fourth pound walnuts, minced together fine and mixed with salad dressing. Spread on rye bread or graham bread, with lettuce leaves between. One cup chopped celery, six stoned olives and two tablespoons salted nuts, minced together with salad dressing. Salted almonds rolled fine and mixed to a paste with butter are nice on crackers, with a chafing dish lunch. Bone sardines and mash them to a paste with lemon juice or oil and spread on thinly sliced bread. Mince canned lobster, shrimp or crabs fine, mix with minced hard boiled eggs and salad dressing and spread between buttered slices of bread.

ANCHOVY SARDINES.—Spread small triangles of bread or toast with anchovy paste. Serve either hot or cold. No top crust for these. Pass lemon slices.

CAVIAR SANDWICHES.—Spread thin slices of rye bread with caviar and sprinkle with finely minced young onions or onion juice. No top crust for these. Serve with lemon points.

CHEESE WAFERS.—Grate cheese and spread it on buttered cracker wafers or buttered wafers of toast and sprinkle lightly with salt and cayenne pepper. Melt cheese in the oven and serve hot.

BOILED EGG SANDWICHES.—Run hard boiled eggs through meat grinder and mix with dry mustard, salt, cayenne pepper and lemon juice or vinegar. Spread between thin slices of buttered bread. Minced celery or celery seed is nice mixed with this paste. The grated rind of a lemon added to ground hard boiled eggs (three), one half cup butter, two tablespoons of lemon juice, salt and half teaspoon of dry mustard makes a good devil paste for sandwiches.

OLIVE AND COTTAGE CHEESE SANDWICHES.—Stone olives, or use the stuffed olives, and chop them fine; mix with an equal quantity of cottage cheese. Make into a smooth paste with soft butter. Spread between graham or rye bread slices. Olives may be mixed likewise with grated cream cheese.

CUCUMBER SANDWICHES.—Use the fresh, sliced cucumbers or cucumber pickles chopped fine. Mix with mayonnaise salad dressing and spread on buttered bread, cover with shredded lettuce and lay slice of buttered bread on top.

WALNUT AND CHEESE SANDWICHES.—Chop walnuts fine and mix with grated cream cheese and a little lemon juice or with soft butter or salad dressing. Spread on lettuce leaves and place between buttered slices of bread.

CELERY SANDWICHES.—Mince celery fine; mix it with chopped nuts and chopped olives and blend together with mayonnaise dressing. Spread between slices of buttered bread.

CHEESE SANDWICHES.—Mix grated cheese with the grated yolks of hard boiled eggs and add a few drops of lemon juice. For a change a few canned, sweet red peppers, chopped fine are nice added to the mixture. Spread between thin slices of buttered white bread.

COTTAGE CHEESE SANDWICHES.—Spread cottage cheese between thin slices of buttered graham, whole wheat or rye bread. Chopped dill pickles are nice mixed with this cheese and spread on rye bread.

NUT AND CHEESE SANDWICHES.—Grate cream cheese and mix it with ground salted peanuts. Make into a paste with butter or thick cream. Spread on graham bread.

DUTCH LUNCH SANDWICH.—Grate cream cheese or cut up Swiss cheese and spread it on thin slices of buttered rye bread; spread with German prepared mustard and press buttered slices of bread on top. Pass dill pickles.

PEANUT SANDWICHES.—Spread thin slices of Boston brown bread with peanut butter or with ground salted peanuts mixed with butter. White graham bread is also used this way.

CLUB HOUSE SANDWICHES.—Spread bread or toast with butter, lay on a thin slice of cold meat chicken, (white meat preferred), spread with mayonnaise salad dressing then put on a layer of shredded lettuce, covered again with mayonnaise dressing and cover top with another thin slice of buttered bread or buttered hot toast. The sliced meat and bread must be cut very thin to make dainty sandwiches of this delicious combination. Garnish with quartered dill pickles and olives or pimentos and parsley.

HOT EGG SANDWICH.—Toast bread in thin slices; lay on a thin slice of hot boiled bacon or ham and upon this place a hot fried egg or an egg scrambled fine. Lay another hot slice of toast on top and serve.

MINCED MEAT SANDWICHES.—Minced cooked chicken or veal, mixed with minced celery and then with mayonnaise dressing is the usual paste for meat sandwiches. The flavor may be varied by adding minced sweet pickles, sweet canned peppers, olives, pimentos, mushrooms or nuts to this paste as fancy dictates. Minced boiled ham and boiled chicken in equal portions make a nice combination. If mayonnaise isn't liked bind together with soft butter, thick cream, lemon juice or prepared mustard.

LAYER SANDWICHES.—These are made of different varieties of bread combined in the same sandwich or of two or more kinds of thinly sliced cold, cooked meat, placed in alternate layers between slices of buttered bread or toast. Cold roast duck, either wild or tame, sliced thinly and placed between buttered slices of raisin bread is nice. Duck may first be dipped in mayonnaise. Cold boiled tongue sliced thin and covered with lettuce mayonnaise and then with a thin slice of chicken or cold boiled ham, make a good layer sandwich. Flaked white fish, spread with minced shrimp mayonnaise and lettuce or minced celery is another. Brown bread and white bread cut as thin as wafers, buttered and spread with cream or cottage cheese and minced olives or nuts and put together in alternate layers then cut through like layer cake into oblong strips or finger sandwiches make pretty luncheon sandwiches. Nut bread and raisin or date bread, sliced, buttered and built in layer sandwiches are delicious. Rings of Boston brown bread alternated with rings of white bread and spread with peanut butter is another popular combination.

SWEET SANDWICHES.—Chop figs, raisins and stoned dates together and spread on buttered slices of graham or white bread. Dates minced with nuts and spread on thin slices of buttered bread or upon cracker wafers make dainty afternoon tea sandwiches. Grated sweet chocolate and ground nuts mixed smooth with butter or cream is another filling. Grated cocoanut and dates minced to a paste is another favorite filling.

GAME SANDWICHES.—Cut thin slices of prairie chicken, wild duck or goose or venison. Dip shredded celery into mayonnaise dressing; lay the sliced meat on buttered bread, scatter shredded celery over it and press bread on top. With sliced venison spread currant jelly on the meat and omit the salad dressing. With sliced turkey use cranberry jelly. With boiled ham cider jelly, grape jelly or apple jelly is nice. With sliced roast veal tomato jelly is best. With wild fowl use mild plum jelly or currant jelly.—Contributed.

HICKORY NUT AND BANANA SANDWICHES.—Slice two bananas and mix with one half cupful of chopped hickory nut meats or pecans. Spread between thin slices of buttered brown bread.

APPLE AND CELERY SANDWICHES.—Mince celery fine and mix with chopped apples, sprinkle lightly with salt and spread between slices of buttered brown bread.

NUT SANDWICHES.—Waldorf. Chop fine equal quantities of sour apples, celery and pecans or other nuts. Salt them, spread on buttered bread, then spread lightly with mayonnaise dressing and make into sandwiches with brown bread.

SMOKED DUCK SANDWICHES.—Cut thin slices from smoked breasts of duck or goose. Cut hard boiled eggs into thin rings, lay over the duck and squeeze lemon juice on them; sprinkle with salt and pepper and place between buttered slices of bread, rye bread preferred.

SMOKED SALMON SANDWICHES.—Cut thin slices of bread, butter it and lay a thin slice of smoked salmon between them, or mash the salmon smooth with minced hard boiled egg and mix with butter to a paste and spread on bread.

BEAN SANDWICHES.—Spread buttered brown bread with cold baked beans, sprinkle with chopped pickles or with salted water cress or nasturtium leaves minced fine.

PICQUANT SANDWICHES.—Garden cress or pepper grass dipped lightly in salt and spread between thin slices of buttered bread makes dainty picquant sandwiches. Minced nasturtium leaves are used likewise.

FRUIT SANDWICHES.—Mince seeded malaga grapes, sliced canned pineapple and mashed bananas together to a paste. Spread on slices of plain white or graham bread or on nut bread. Cover with a thin layer of salad dressing and press thin sliced buttered bread on top.

DIXIE SANDWICHES.—Spread sliced nut bread with butter and grated cream cheese, or with melted cream cheese and press buttered bread on top.

RAISIN SANDWICHES.—Spread raisin bread slices with grated cheese and cover with a slice of buttered raisin bread.

NUT AND CHOCOLATE SANDWICHES.—Spread thin slices of buttered nut bread with chocolate fudge or fondant. Raisin bread is nice used the same way.

MARSHMALLOW SANDWICHES.—Toast marshmallows and place between thin slices of buttered nut bread. Mushrooms may be steamed with a little cream, spread on buttered bread and covered with a thin coating of chocolate fudge or fondant. Set the fondant dish in hot water to melt it for spreading.

Salads

"How in the name of thrift does he rake this together?"—Shakespeare.

SALAD DRESSING.—One cup sugar, one tablespoonful salt, pinch cayenne pepper, one tablespoonful mustard, stir all together. Add four eggs beaten, one cup cream, add one cup butter, put on fire in double boiler. When it boils remove and beat in one half pint vinegar a little at a time. This will keep till used.—Mrs. C. C. Mackenroth.

SALAD DRESSING.—Yolks of six eggs, two tablespoons butter, three fourths cup sugar, two thirds cup vinegar, two teaspoons mustard, one half teaspoon salt. Mix sugar, salt and mustard then add butter. Mix until smooth. Lastly add beaten yolks and vinegar. Cook until thick.—Mrs. F. Kleinsorge.

SALAD DRESSING.—Yolks of four eggs, one half cup vinegar, two tablespoons sugar, butter the size of walnut, salt and pepper to taste. Beat yolks until light, add sugar and beat again, then add vinegar, butter, salt and pepper. Cook in double boiler until quite thick stirring all the while. When cold thin with cream. A very little flour may be added while cooking. This will keep for several days. Adding cream only as you use it.—Mrs. McGuiness.

A Group of Salad Dressings

OIL MAYONNAISE.—Mix the yolk of one raw egg, one half teaspoon of salt, a little mustard and a few grains of cayenne, add one cup of oil in small portions, and two tablespoons lemon juice. Make as you would any mayonnaise dressing, and when ready to serve stir in one half cup of sour cream.—Contributed.

SOUR CREAM SALAD DRESSING.—Stir one tablespoon of sugar, one half teaspoon of salt, one fourth teaspoon of pepper and one tablespoon of lemon juice into one cup of sour cream. Serve it on cucumbers, onions, cabbage or lettuce.—Contributed.

FRENCH DRESSING.—With many people the French dressing is usually hit or miss. There is, however, a set formula that ensures having the proportions right every time. Put into a bowl or bottle a half teaspoonful salt, and a salt spoonful of pepper. Add four tablespoonfuls olive oil, stir with a fork or shake it in a bottle. Add one tablespoonful of lemon juice or vinegar, mix thoroughly and pour over the salad. Tarragon vinegar may be substituted in whole or part of the cider or white wine vinegar.—Contributed.

ENGLISH SALAD DRESSING.—Mash the yolks of two hard boiled eggs to a paste. Add a saltspoonful of salt, a scant teaspoonful of powdered sugar, a few grains cayenne; a teaspoonful of cold water and mix it well. Stir in by degrees a half cupful of cream, then stirring very rapidly, add a tablespoonful of strong Chili vinegar and one of cider vinegar. Six tablespoonfuls of olive oil may be used instead of cream, adding gradually.—Contributed.

CHICKEN SALAD.—Boil a chicken tender in salted water, cut the meat into small pieces; add half as much diced celery or chopped cabbage. Mix with salad dressing. Add one cupful of broken English walnuts just before serving.

SALAD DRESSING.—Yolks of five eggs and one whole one, beaten with one large tablespoon of sugar, one teaspoon of mustard, dash salt and cayenne pepper. Cook thick in one half cup of hot vinegar and three tablespoons of butter. Remove from fire and beat smooth. When ready to serve thin with half a cup of sweet cream.—Mrs. Fred Southard.

APPLE SALAD.—One cup chopped celery, two cups of chopped apples, one half cup of nuts. Mix and serve with salad dressing.—Mrs. Southard.

SALMON SALAD.—One large can of salmon, four hard boiled eggs minced with salmon. Mix with salad dressing.—Mrs. Southard. (Editorial note.—Above recipes for salads were demonstrated by Mrs. Southard in her paper on "Salads" for Domestic Science club.)

CHICKEN SALAD.—Cut cooked chicken into dice and add half as much diced celery. Mix with half of salad dressing and pour the balance over it at serving time. Dressing: Yolks of four eggs, one teaspoon of salt, one heaping teaspoon of sugar, one teaspoon mustard, one cup weak vinegar and speck of cayenne. Cook thick in double boiler. When cold add one cup of whipped cream.—Mrs. W. S. Davidson.

SHRIMP SALAD.—One can of shrimps, wash thoroughly, then pick to pieces; two cups cabbage sliced fine; two cups chopped celery, one cup English walnuts cut quite fine. Mix together and serve with salad dressing.

SALAD DRESSING.—Yolks of five eggs and one whole egg well beaten, one tablespoon sugar, six tablespoonfuls of vinegar and three of butter boiled together and turned slowly over beaten eggs, one tablespoonful of dry mustard, one teaspoonful of salt, dash of red pepper. Cook in double boiler until thick. When wanted for table add whipped cream.—Mrs. T. A. McKay.

LOBSTER SALAD.—One cup of chopped celery, five hard boiled eggs coarsely diced, one large or two small cans of lobster coarsely shredded, season with salt and a dash of cayenne, mix lightly with fork. Dressing for above: One half cup vinegar, one teaspoon mustard, one half teaspoon salt, three tablespoons melted butter, three level tablespoons of sugar. Cook in double boiler. When well heated add well beaten yolks of four eggs and one whole egg, stirring continuously till thick and smooth. When ready to mix with salad thin to proper consistency with sweet or sour cream, place salad on lettuce and pour dressing over it.—Mrs. Harry McKay.

SHRIMP SALAD.—One can shrimps, one small head celery, one cucumber, cut all into dice. Dressing: Yolks of two eggs; pinch of salt; dash of cayenne pepper. Beat well. Have olive oil very cold and pour it in and keep beating until it gets thick. Then add either vinegar or lemon juice. Mix with shrimps, just before serving.—Mrs. Will Lynch.

HAZELS HERRING SALAD.—Take equal quantities of cold boiled potatoes and herring and two or three small onions. Cut potatoes in cubes, remove bones from herring and cut in small pieces or pick to pieces, add onions and let stand on ice till ready to serve, cover with sweet cream and season with salt and pepper.—Mrs. Schollander.

POTATO SALAD.—I do not know much about salads different from the every day style, with the exception of an old fashioned German potato salad. Boil your potatoes with the jackets, peel and slice while hot; heat bacon drippings in which glaze onions which must be cut very fine, then add flour, brown, add diluted vinegar, let it come to a boil, cool, add a little sweet cream, turn it over your potatoes, which were previously seasoned with pepper and salt. Garnish with either sliced or chopped hard boiled eggs and green parsley.

STRING BEAN SALAD.—Cut ends of tender green beans, string them, cut them either lengthwise, or just break them, boil until tender, add salt, drain. Slice onion very fine, mix with beans, season with pepper, and another pinch of salt, pour diluted vinegar over them, turn diced fried bacon quite hot over this mixture.

CABBAGE SALAD OR DUTCH SLAW.—Select a nice clean cabbage, slice very fine, something like sauer kraut; place in a stew pan, pour boiling water on, let stand for half hour, then drain, slice onion fine, mix with cabbage, season with salt and pepper, turn over this hot bacon grease, with bacon dices in diluted vinegar. Above vegetable salads were given by Mrs. Bruegger in her German Cookery demonstration.

BEET AND CHEESE SALAD.—Make cottage cheese into balls, stick on either side half English walnut. Slice small sweet beets and put two cheese balls and three beet slices on lettuce leaf. Keep on ice until just before time to serve. Add French dressing just before serving. This is a simple salad and so tasty that you will be sure to like it.

FRENCH DRESSING.—Mix three teaspoonfuls of cider vinegar with three and one half tablespoonfuls of olive oil, one large pinch of salt, one tiny pinch of black pepper and red pepper.

TOMATO SALAD.—Choose smooth, red tomatoes, peel; cut into halves, set on ice. Dip each piece into vinegar, lay on lettuce leaf. Drop a spoonful of mayonnaise on each and garnish with nasturtiums.—Mrs. R. J. Walker.

SPINACH SALAD.—Chop cold boiled spinach fine, season well with salt and pepper, and a little nutmeg and mould into small cups. When cold and formed, turn out on lettuce leaves and garnish with hard boiled eggs sliced or the yolks of hard boiled eggs run through a ricer. Serve with mayonnaise. Strips of Spanish red peppers may be used for garnishing in place of the eggs. The nutmeg can be omitted if distasteful, but most people find it an attractive addition.—Contributed.

SHRIMP AND TOMATO SALAD.—Add to the contents of one can of shrimps, an equal amount of crisp white celery cut in small pieces. Mix with a cream or mayonnaise dressing. Place a thick slice of tomato on a crisp lettuce leaf, and a mound of the salad mixture on the tomato. Decorate with a few stuffed olives on each serving, and top with a spoonful of the mayonnaise. If ripe tomatoes are too expensive or not obtainable at this season the salad may be served on tomato jelly cut in thick slices or else molded in the form of cups.—Contributed.

TOMATO JELLY.—To make the tomato jelly salad, soak a quarter cupful of gelatine in the same amount of water. When softened put into a sauce pan with a cupful of strained tomato, a quarter cupful cold water, a teaspoonful of salt, the same amount of onion juice, a tablespoonful of tarragon vinegar, and a quarter teaspoonful of white pepper. Stir over the fire until the gelatine is dissolved, but not a moment longer, turn at once into egg cups or small molds and set away to harden. Serve on lettuce leaves with mayonnaise.—Contributed.

TOMATO SALAD WITH MAYONNAISE.—Have as many hallowed out tomatoes or molded tomatoes as there are guests to serve and set each in a crisp lettuce leaf. Upon this lay half of an egg that has been deviled and with this three little silvery sardines. Sprinkle with pieces of green pepper, cut fine and dress with mayonnaise.—Contributed.

FANCY EGG SALAD.—Select perfect lettuce leaves and arrange in circles on a large platter or on individual plates. Cut hard boiled eggs into halves, remove the yolks and cut the whites into petals shaped like water lilies. Arrange these strips in the center of the lettuce leaves (which simulate lily pads) to form a circle, leaving a small circular opening in the middle. Then put in a second row of petals, placing the pieces between those in the first circle. Lastly press the egg yolks through a ricer, heaping them in the center of the white petals, to represent the heart of a lily. Pass a bowl of mayonnaise with the salad or heap lightly on the surface.—Contributed.

POTATO SALAD.—Boil six medium sized potatoes in jackets, until done but do not let them break into pieces. They should be firm and dry. Peel them and cut into thin slices or small dice; mix with two small onions chopped and two hard boiled eggs, sliced. Mix thoroughly with boiled salad dressing, after dressing the potatoes first with lemon juice or vinegar and salt. Let stand on the ice an hour or more. Garnish the salad bowl with shredded lettuce, diced, boiled or pickled beets or radish roses or olives, sweet peppers or any favorite garnish.—Contributed.

FRENCH DINNER SALAD.—The dinner salad should always be delicate and light. Heavy meat or fish salads are reserved for luncheon or buffet suppers, where they form the main dish of the meal. The most popular dinner salad is lettuce dressed with oil and lemon juice or vinegar. Cress is often used and of late years bleached dandelions are much in favor. Sliced cucumbers and onion, or sliced tomatoes with shredded lettuce or chopped celery, and the typical spring salad of shredded lettuce, sliced young onions and sliced radishes are all liked. In France the French dressing of oil and vinegar or lemon juice is always used but in America many prefer the richer mayonnaise dressing. In any case the salad is never mixed until time to serve it, and then the dressing should be lightly tossed in when all of the ingredients must be crisp and cold.—Contributed.

PIMENTO SALAD.—Select sweet, red or green peppers, steam them till the skin cracks, then skin and seed. Place on the ice and shred with cold boiled fish, or shell fish or with a mixture of cold, cooked and diced potatoes, green peas or beans and sliced cucumbers or celery. The canned sweet red peppers or pimentos may be substituted. Spiced or pickled green peppers are also nice with a crisp green salad.—Mrs. Whitehead.

Vegetables

"Dyspepsia is largely the result of trying to force square meals into round stomachs."

TIME FOR BOILING VEGETABLES.—Turnips should be peeled and boiled from forty minutes to one hour. Beets; boil from one to two hours then put in cold water then slip the skin off. Spinach; boil twenty minutes in uncovered kettle if green color is to be retained. Parsnips; boil from twenty to thirty minutes. String beans should be boiled one and one half hours, covered. Shelled beans require one hour to cook. Onions should be boiled from forty minutes to one hour, covered. Green corn; boil ten to twenty minutes. Green peas should be boiled in very little water, boil twenty minutes. Asparagus should be cooked the same as peas. Serve on toast with cream gravy or melted butter. Cabbage should be boiled from one to two hours in plenty of salted water. Carrots should be boiled from forty minutes to one hour. Whole potatoes should be put in boiling salted water and boil rapidly in covered kettle from fifteen to thirty minutes according to size and age. Test with the tines of a fork. Drain as soon as tender, remove the cover and set on back of range to dry. If they are to be mashed do not let them stand long.

VEGETABLES.—Vegetables of all kinds should be thoroughly picked over and well washed, and it is good sometimes to lay them into cold water a short time before cooking. Salt should not be added until partly cooked, as it has a tendency to harden them; they should cook steadily, do not allow them to stop boiling or simmering until they are thoroughly done. Drain, take some butter, heat it, add a little flour, mix smooth in the butter, add milk enough to make a smooth gravy, turn over vegetables, and let it heat through, then serve. This sauce is nice for many kinds. For asparagus, carrots, peas and a few others I keep some of the liquid they were boiled in, as it gives them a better flavor than milk alone.

GERMAN CABBAGE.—Another way of preparing cabbage in a German way: Cut up a cabbage and pick over carefully, wash well, heat some lard, drop cabbage into the hot grease, stir, so as to get it all heated, then let fry for a short time, but watch carefully to avoid burning, then add a quartered cooking apple; now when it gets too dry add hot water from the tea kettle, and let it simmer for three or four hours, the longer the better, add salt when almost tender, and about half hour before serving add quarter cup of sugar, quarter cup of vinegar, and let simmer the last half hour. This is the real German way.

GREEN STRING BEANS.—Select tender green string beans, cut the ends and remove strings, dice and wash thoroughly, put on in cold water to cover, add salt when partly cooked, then diced potatoes, and boil with beans about half an hour. Then heat either bacon drippings or common lard, add flour and brown, when ready turn the beans, potatoes, liquor and all into the hot mixture, add a little vinegar and pepper. Summer savory sprigs added to above give it a fine flavor.—Mrs. George Bruegger, German Cookery demonstration of vegetables.

CREAMED POTATOES.—Cut cold boiled potatoes into one half inch cubes, put these in a sauce pan. Add white sauce and finely cut parsley. Serve.

WHITE SAUCE.—Two tablespoons butter, two tablespoons flour, one cup milk, salt and pepper. Rub flour and butter together with spoon in sauce pan, add milk, add salt and pepper and potatoes. Cook thick.—Dorothy Whitehead.

STUFFED POTATOES.—Bake the desired number of potatoes, cut open the top, scoop out inside, mash. Add butter, salt and pepper, moisten with hot milk or cream to taste and add beaten whites of two eggs. Fill skin with this mixture, heap well, brush over with yolk of egg and brown in oven. Serve hot.—Mrs. R. J. Walker.

STUFFED CABBAGE.—One large cabbage, two pounds beef chopped fine, one half cup melted butter, one half cup sweet cream or milk, one half teaspoon ginger, one half teaspoon allspice, salt and pepper to suit taste, whites of two eggs beaten stiff. Cut the stem end off the cabbage far enough down to form a cover, scoop out enough of the center of the cabbage to allow room for the meat. Mix the meat and other ingredients together and place in the cabbage, put on the cover, tie in a cloth and boil for three hours, or until the cabbage is done, in salt water.

SAUCE.—Two thirds cup butter, one half teaspoon each of ginger and allspice; salt and pepper to suit taste, and one quart milk, thicken with flour.—Mrs. Aaron J. Bessie.

NORWEGIAN SAUERKRAUT.—One medium sized head of cabbage cut in fine long strips with a knife, put in kettle, to this add three quarters of an ounce of flour sprinkled over the top of cabbage, one teaspoon salt, one teaspoon caraway seed, one pint beef broth. Let this boil slowly until tender, stir every few minutes to keep the cabbage from burning. When done add one teaspoon sugar and one teaspoon vinegar.—Mrs. R. Meidell.

STEWED OKRA AND TOMATO (CREOLE).—Twelve pods of okra sliced thin, four tomatoes sliced. Stew with salt and pepper and butter, half an hour slowly, add dash cayenne pepper and serve.

SOUTHERN SWEET POTATOES.—Slice cold boiled sweet potatoes. Lay in a buttered baking dish, sprinkle with sugar and dot with butter. Bake Brown.—Mrs. Whitehead, Southern Cookery demonstration.

SCALLOPED SWEET POTATOES.—Boil six sweet potatoes in salted water and cut them into thin slices in a baking dish. Mix with a well seasoned cream sauce, cover with fine bread crumbs and dot with butter. Brown in the oven.

POTATO SOUFFLE.—Four good sized potatoes boiled and mashed fine, one half teacup of milk, one tablespoon butter. Let butter and milk come to a scald, add potatoes, a little salt and pepper, beat to a cream, add slowly the beaten yolks of four eggs. Beat the whites to a stiff froth, add them to the mixture. Do not beat often adding the white of egg. Bake twenty minutes in a brisk oven. Serve while hot with meats that have gravy.—Mrs. Mary Harvey.

COLD SLAW.—This is a creole dish and very delicious. Cut very fine a quarter of a head of firm white cabbage. Put it into a covered dish, pour over it one half cupful of vinegar, one half tablespoonful of salt and toss it about lightly with a fork. Into a skillet pour one half cupful of milk, a teaspoonful of butter and one quarter of a cupful of sugar. Beat one egg light. Let the milk come to a boil, mix a teaspoonful of the milk with the egg, add sugar and butter, allow it to cook until a custard is formed, then pour over the sliced cabbage. Allow it to become very cold before using. As vinegars differ do not use so much if very strong.—Mrs. A. McKay.

CANNED STRING BEANS.—Prepare the beans as for dinner—that is, string and break into one inch pieces. Have your cans and top all cleansed; then fill the cans with the beans—after washing them, of course—and shake them down. Put one teaspoonful of salt to a quart of beans after the cans are full. Now put fresh cold water upon them to overflowing. I run a thin knife between the can and the beans to get all the air bubbles out. Put on the rubbers and then the lids, but not tight—only as you can with the thumb and one finger. Lay thin boards in the bottom of the boiler and set your can on them; fill to the lids with cold water. I let them boil two hours after they are fairly at it; then I take them out one by one, and screw down the tops and set to get cold before putting away. When we eat them I drain off all the water, put in a piece of butter and pepper and milk, or any way I want them. I never lost a can.—Contributed.

NUT LOAF.—Two cupfuls bread crumbs, one cup chopped walnuts, one half cup butter, one cup strained tomatoes, one small grated onion, one egg, salt and pepper to taste. Pack in a can and steam one hour.—Mrs. A. McKay.

POTATOES A LA MAITRE D'HOTEL.—Two cups potato balls or cubes, one cup hot milk, three level tablespoons butter, yolk of one egg, one half level teaspoon salt, one eighth level teaspoon paprika, one teaspoon lemon juice, one level teaspoon chopped parsley. Cook the potato in boiling salted water until tender. Drain and put into double boiler; add milk and cook until it is nearly absorbed. Cream the butter, add to it the egg yolk slightly beaten, add the salt, paprika and lemon juice. Stir this mixture into the potatoes and as soon as cooked turn into a hot dish, sprinkle with the parsley and serve.—Contributed.

HOMINY FRITTERS.—Break up two cups of cold cooked hominy with a fork. Add one scant cup of milk, a pinch of salt, one beaten egg and one half cup of flour in which one level teaspoon of baking powder is sifted. Drop by spoonfuls into hot lard and fry until a delicate brown.—Contributed.

TOMATO SOUFFLE.—One can tomatoes, two level tablespoons butter, two level tablespoons flour, one half teaspoon salt, one eighth level teaspoon paprika, one teaspoon onion juice, one fourth cup fine bread crumbs, three eggs. Drain the tomatoes and cook the liquid down to one cup. Cut the tomatoes into small pieces using one cup free from seeds. Melt the butter. Add the flour, salt and paprika and when blended add the cup of tomato liquid. Stir until thick and smooth. Add the onion juice, tomato and the bread crumbs. Remove from the fire, and add the yolks of the eggs beaten very light. Then fold in the white beaten stiff. Pour into a buttered baking dish and bake in a moderate oven until light and firm in the center.—Contributed.

POTATO CROQUETTES.—Prepare one pint of hot mashed potatoes seasoned with one tablespoonful of butter, one half teaspoonful of salt, one half teaspoonful onion juice. Beat all together until very light, and when slightly cool add the yolk of one egg. Mix well and put through a sieve to be sure there are no lumps, as it is almost impossible to get them out by mashing the potato. And one teaspoonful of chopped parsley. Shape into smooth round balls. Roll them in bread crumbs, then dip into beaten egg, then roll them in crumbs again. Fry in smoking hot lard one minute, drain on soft paper and serve in the form of a pyramid.—Contributed.

MUSHROOM AND POTATO CROQUETTES.—Take one pound of mushrooms (the fresh are preferred to the canned), break in small pieces after rinsing, drop into three tablespoonfuls of hot butter, dust with half a teaspoonful of salt and a trifle of pepper, cover and steam slowly for ten minutes; add to three small cupfuls of seasoned mashed potato, beat in two eggs and a tablespoonful of chopped parsley: form into cones, egg and crumb and fry in hot fat.

GERMAN FRIED POTATOES.—Or fried raw potatoes make an appetizing dish for breakfast. Slice raw potatoes as thin as an egg shell and put them into a frying pan in which an equal amount of butter and lard is boiling. Sprinkle them over with salt and pepper and cover with a close fitting lid and let the steam partly cook them. Fry until golden color.

FRENCH SPINACH.—Boil one half peck spinach until tender in salted water. Drain, throw into a colander and drench well with cold water. This gives it a certain firmness and delicacy. Shake free from water, chop fine and put in a hot sauce pan, salt delicately and heat with butter and cream. Then heap in a vegetable dish and garnish with poached or boiled eggs.

WILTED LETTUCE.—Pick fresh, young garden lettuce when it is just big enough to eat. Wash it and shred it, sprinkle with salt, pepper and a little sugar. Minced young green onions may be mixed with it if liked. Cut four or five slices of bacon into cubes or as much ham and fry it brown in its own grease. Add two tablespoons of vinegar and the yolk of an egg beaten together and heat in the grease; turn hot over the prepared lettuce and stir quickly with a fork. Same dressing is nice on young cooked string beans.—Mrs. Whitehead.

BUTTERED ASPARAGUS.—Cut the tough ends from a bunch of asparagus (white variety preferred) or the canned may be used. Leave it in five inch stalks and boil it tender in salted water. Drain, melt three fourths cup of butter. Lay the asparagus on individual serving plates, and pour the butter generously over it, or it may be served on toast. Two tablespoons of thick cream added is liked by many, especially when the fresh asparagus is used. Asparagus is nice served in the same manner, cold, with sauce tartar or a thick mayonnaise dressing heaped at one side of the plate. Dip each stalk in it as it is eaten.—Mrs. Whitehead.

SCALLOPED CABBAGE.—Chop a head of cabbage quite coarse. Boil it twenty minutes in salted water, drain. Make a cream sauce and add to the cabbage, cover with bread crumbs and bake. For varieties take and sprinkle the top thickly with grated cheese and serve cabbage au gratin.—Contributed.

CORN SOUFFLE.—One pint of fresh or canned corn cooked in one cup of milk ten minutes. Season with salt, pepper, one teaspoon of sugar and one teaspoon of butter. Let it get cold, then add beaten yolks of three eggs and lastly cut in the stiffly beaten whites of the eggs and bake in a buttered pudding dish.—Contributed.

BEETS.—Boil young beets tender in water to cover. Drain and cover with cold water then skin them and slice fine. Heat half cup diluted vinegar, salt, pepper and butter, turn over the prepared beets and serve.—Contributed.

GREEN BEANS (GERMAN).—String the beans and shred into lengthwise strips. Cook in salted water until tender, then drain and add some vinegar dressing as for beets. Serve either hot or cold.—Contributed.

BOILED STRING BEANS AND BACON.—Fill a kettle with green or wax beans, shredded or broken into inch lengths, insert a piece of bacon or salt pork (about one pound) in the center of the beans, cover with cold water and boil gently two or three hours covering the kettle. Add more salt, if necessary and a good dash of pepper. Let the water about cook off the beans and serve either hot or cold. Fresh pork may be used with equal success.

Pickles, Condiments and Spiced Fruits

"Mingle, mingle, mingle, you that mingle, may."

RIPE CUCUMBER PICKLES.—Pare and seed ripe cucumbers, slice lengthwise and cut into pieces desired size. Let them stand twenty-four hours covered with cold vinegar. Drain, then put in fresh vinegar with two pounds of sugar and one ounce of cassia buds to one quart of vinegar and a tablespoonful of salt. Boil all together twenty minutes. Put in a crock and cover closely.—Mrs. W. C. Lynch.

GREEN TOMATOES AND ONIONS.—One peck of green tomatoes sliced, and use about one half as many onions as tomatoes and to this quantity add three peppers (either green or red) cut in small pieces. Sprinkle lightly with salt and let stand over night. Drain off liquor and when dry put them in hot vinegar which has been sweetened and spiced with cinnamon and cloves. Boil until tender. Leave spice bag in jar.—Mrs. Lynch.

UNCOOKED MUSTARD PICKLES.—(Excellent). Four quarts small cucumbers, four quarts small onions, three heads cauliflower, six green peppers. Dressing: One gallon of vinegar, two pounds of brown sugar, one pound mustard, one cup of flour. Let pickles stand over night in mild brine. Drain and put in jar. Then make dressing as follows and pour boiling hot over them. Boil vinegar and sugar together and thicken with flour dissolved in cold water. Pour this while boiling over pickles, when cold add mustard which has been dissolved in cold vinegar.—Mrs. Lynch.

CHILI SAUCE (Very nice).—One quart onions, two quarts cabbage, two quarts tomatoes, green, two quarts cucumbers, two quarts mangoes, one quart celery. Soak the tomatoes over night in salt water, run all the vegetables through food chopper and scald all together in clear water ten minutes then drain this water off. Mix one half cup flour, one and one half cups sugar, ten cents worth of mustard seeds, five cents worth of turmeric powder, five cents worth of celery seeds, two quarts vinegar. Pour over all and boil fifteen minutes. This has to be put in sealed jars.—Mrs. Southard.

CURRANT CATSUP.—Five pounds currants, three pounds sugar, one half pint vinegar, one teaspoonful cloves, one teaspoonful cinnamon, one teaspoonful salt, one teaspoonful allspice, one teaspoonful black and red pepper mixed. Boil one half hour and seal.—Mrs. Davidson.

SPICED CURRANTS.—Four pounds currants, five pounds sugar, one pint vinegar, two tablespoons cinnamon, two tablespoons cloves, two tablespoons allspice. Boil until thick.—Mrs. Mary Harvey.

CHUTNEY SAUCE.—One half pound brown sugar, eight tomatoes, eight ounces raisins, one quarter ounce cayenne pepper, one quarter ounce ginger, three ounces garlic, four ounces salt, one quart of vinegar. Boil all to a mush for several hours.—Mrs. Schollander.

GREEN APPLE CHUTNEY.—Pare and core six pounds of greening apples; boil in one quart of vinegar; set off until cool. Boil two pounds of moist brown sugar in one pint of vinegar; add two pounds of Sultana raisins, washed, picked and dried and four ounces of garlic pounded with vinegar; four ounces of green ginger; two ounces of red pepper and four ounces of salt. Mix well together with more vinegar if too thick. Keep on the back of the stove one day, slowly simmering, stirring occasionally with a wooden spoon. Bottle on the next day.

ORIENTAL CHUTNEY.—Peel and core three pounds of tart apples. Mix with a pound of stoned tamarinds, three quarters of a pound of seeded raisins, a head of garlic, two pods of red pepper, and one ounce of grated ginger roots. Pound all together until reduced to a pulp. Add to the mixture a pint of brown sugar and a tablespoon each of currant jelly and thick tomato catsup. Blend well with a wooden spoon. Put in small jars and seal. This chutney improves with age and is most pungent.

EAST INDIA CHUTNEY.—Into three pints vinegar put a bag containing two ounces of ground mustard, four ounces of mustard seed, one ounce of cayenne pepper and one quarter ounce of turmeric. Add a pound of brown sugar and scant half pound of salt. Chop together thirteen large ripe apples, one pound of seeded raisins, seven large ripe tomatoes, four small onions and two cloves of garlic. Mince fine. Boil in the vinegar mixture for two hours. Press through a colander and bottle while hot. This is fine for cold meat, particularly so with roast pork.

GREEN GOOSEBERRY CHUTNEY.—This relish has not yet become common in America, though it is found on all well supplied English tables. Four pounds green gooseberries (not too ripe), one half ounce cayenne pepper, two ounces garlic, two ounces dried ginger, three pounds loaf sugar, two ounces mustard seed, two scant quarts best vinegar. Put the berries, when picked over, into a preserving kettle with one quart of vinegar and sugar and let simmer for an hour; pound the seeds, garlic, etc., and add, stirring with wooden spoon; when well mixed add more vinegar until the mass is of the proper consistency for chutney. Cool and bottle.

CORN SALAD.—Take one dozen ears of corn, (cut corn from cobs), one large head of cabbage chopped quite fine, not quite a half box of mustard, one cup sugar, one tablespoon chopped peppers, two tablespoons salt, mix with about four cups of good vinegar and boil about ten minutes, first mix the mustard with some of the vinegar. If too thick when done add more vinegar. Put in jars while hot. Will keep all winter, very nice with meat and potatoes.—Mrs. Paul Leonhardy.

MIXED PICKLES.—Two quarts green tomatoes chopped, one quart cabbage chopped, one quart onions chopped, two green peppers chopped, one quart brown sugar, one tablespoon each of cinnamon, cloves, celery seed, white mustard seed. Salt to taste. Boil about twenty minutes.—Mrs. D. E. Plier.

PRESERVED GREEN TOMATOES.—Take one peck of green tomatoes, peel and slice them, slice four lemons without removing the skins, put to this quantity six pounds of granulated sugar, and boil until transparent, and the syrup thick.—Mrs. George Bruegger.

OIL PICKLES.—(Sliced). Slice but do not pare medium sized cucumbers, sufficient to fill a gallon jar. Sprinkle one half cup of salt through the sliced cucumbers and stand in cool place two or three hours, then drain from the salt. Use one ounce black mustard seed, one ounce white mustard seed, one ounce celery seed, or one cup of finely minced celery, one half pint of olive oil, two onions chopped fine. Spread the cucumbers in the jar in layers sprinkling the seeds over them and spreading with part of the olive oil repeating the layers until the jar is filled, then cover all with cold, strained vinegar. Cover and set aside for future use.—Contributed.

SPICED BEETS.—Boil beets tender, lay in cold water, remove skins and unless small, slice and pack in fruit cans. Boil one cup of vinegar, three cups of water, one cup of sugar and spices to suit taste. Pour hot over the beets and seal.—Contributed.

UNCOOKED CHILI SAUCE.—Skin one peck of ripe tomatoes and chop them fine, add two cups skinned and chopped onions, two cups chopped celery, two cups sugar, one cup salt, four tablespoons white mustard seed, two teaspoons ground cloves, six or eight red peppers chopped fine, two teaspoons of ground black pepper and one quart of pure vinegar. Seal in air tight bottle.—Contributed.

PICKLES.—To a gallon of rain water add one cup of salt. Boil it and cover a gallon jar of pickles with the brine, drain off water, bring to a boil and turn over pickles for nine successive mornings. Then take out the pickles, pack in jars with layers of mixed spices. Boil enough vinegar (diluted if very strong) and add one cup of sugar to each gallon of vinegar and add a piece of alum size of a small walnut. Pour hot over the pickles in the jar, cover and put a weight on them and store in a dry, cool place. Good.—Contributed.

EASY PICKLES.—Take pickles of uniform size (about three inches long) wash and pack in fruit jars as tightly as you can. Add one cup of salt, one cup of sugar, an ounce of mixed white and black mustard seed, an ounce of whole cloves and cinnamon bark mixed or any spices preferred and alum the size of a walnut to one gallon of vinegar. Bring to a good boil, then turn over the pickles in the jars and seal. A piece of horse radish root is nice placed in each jar.—Contributed.

WATER MELON PICKLES.—Peel and cut the water melon rind into small cubes and boil it until tender and clear in water to cover, with alum the size of a pea. Drain and boil again in a syrup made of one pint of diluted vinegar and three pints of sugar. Add cloves and cinnamon in spice bag, to suit taste. Pour over the pickles, bring to a boil and cover pickles for three days in succession. Then seal.—Contributed.

CANNED CURRANT JUICE.—Express juice from currants by mashing through colander. Mix one pound of sugar with each pint of juice. Cook five minutes and seal. Use one tablespoon of canned juice to a glass of ice water and fill with crushed ice. Raspberry, strawberry and cherry juices may be canned likewise using a little less sugar.

SPICED GOOSEBERRIES.—Six quarts of gooseberries, four and one half quarts sugar. Boil one hour, add one pint vinegar and one tablespoon each of cloves, cinnamon and allspice. Boil three minutes then seal.

SPICED PLUMS.—Ten pounds of blue plums, eight pounds sugar, one pint vinegar and one tablespoon cloves and cinnamon. Boil to a jam and seal.

SPICED GRAPES.—Pulp seven pounds of grapes by separating skins and pulp and pressing pulp through a colander to extract seeds, then mixing it with the skins. Boil with four and one half pounds of sugar and one teaspoon each of cloves, cinnamon and allspice. Boil twenty minutes or to a soft jam.

SPICED CURRANTS.—To four quarts of ripe currants, add three and one half pounds brown sugar, one pint vinegar and one tablespoon each of cloves and cinnamon. Cook until currants are tender. Boil syrup thick first then adding the currants.

SPICED GREEN TOMATOES.—Chop eight pounds of green tomatoes fine, add four pounds brown sugar, boil three hours then add nearly one quart of vinegar and one teaspoon each of cloves, cinnamon and mace. Boil fifteen minutes and seal.

PEPPER HASH.—(Uncooked.) Chop one head of cabbage, one bunch celery, one half dozen green peppers and one half dozen peeled and sliced onions fine together and let stand over night. Drain in the morning and mix the chopped vegetables with one quart of vinegar, two cups white sugar, one half cup of salt, two tablespoons of mustard seed and one tablespoon of celery seed. Seal in jars, keeps well all winter.—Contributed.

SPICED GOOSEBERRIES AND SPICED CURRANTS.—Make a syrup of three pounds of sugar and one pint of vinegar, add steamed gooseberries (about six pounds) and when cooked thick add one tablespoon of cinnamon and one half tablespoon of cloves and allspice. For spiced currants substitute fresh red currants freed from stems but cook only until the currants are tender as too much boiling makes them hard and tough. Boil the syrup quite thick before adding the currants and then bring to a boil and simmer five minutes.

PICKLED CHERRIES.—Five pounds of stoned cherries, one quart of vinegar, two pounds of sugar, one half ounce each of cinnamon, cloves and mace. Tie spices in a thin bag and boil with the vinegar and sugar to a thick syrup. Pour over the cherries and seal. If the large dark California cherries are used do not stone them.

Cakes

GENERAL DIRECTIONS FOR MAKING CAKE.—Cream the butter and sugar, usually beat the whites and yolks of eggs separately, mix the yolks with the butter and sugar, add the milk, sift the baking powder with the flour and stir in a little at a time then the whites of the eggs, then the flavoring. For cakes containing no butter beat the egg yolks until very light and thick. Add the sugar gradually beating until very light and spongy. Add flavoring and liquid. Have the whites beaten to a stiff froth adding them alternately with the sifted flour (mixed with the baking powder or cream of tartar) and cut both in very lightly.

GOLD CAKE.—Yolks of eight eggs, one and one fourth cups granulated sugar, three fourths cup butter, three fourths cup water, two and one half cups flour, two heaping teaspoons baking powder, one half teaspoon of lemon extract. Sift flour and measure, add baking powder and sift three times. Cream butter and sugar until light and creamy, add yolks beaten light and beat well together, then add water and flavoring and the flour. Beat hard. Bake in greased tin or in layers. Loaf cakes are nicer baked in a funnel cake pan.—Mrs. Fred Southard.

DELICATE CAKE.—One half cup of butter creamed with one cup of sugar until very light, add one half cupful of milk and one and one half cups of flour sifted with one teaspoon of baking powder. Lastly add the flavoring and stiffly beaten whites of four eggs. Bake in one sheet or in two layers and ice with brown carmel or white frosting. Nice for small family. For large layer cake double the recipe.—Mrs. Whitehead.

LULA'S WHITE CAKE.—One and one half cups of sugar creamed with one half cup butter until very light, add one cup of milk alternately with three cups of sifted flour. (Sift flour four times). Whites of six eggs beaten very stiff. When partly beaten add two even teaspoons of cream of tartar to the eggs. Dissolve one even teaspoon of soda in one tablespoon of the milk and add it with the milk. Cut in the beaten whites of eggs last, as you do for sponge cake. Flavor with lemon, vanilla or almond extract as preferred. Bake in a greased funnel tin. Bake twenty minutes in a moderately warm oven, then increase the heat and bake to fifty minutes or until done. Ice with boiled frosting.—Mrs. Whitehead.

GOLD CAKE.—One cup of butter, one and one half cups of sugar, eight yolks of eggs, three cupfuls of pastry flour, one teaspoon of baking powder, one teaspoon of lemon flavor. Cream butter and sugar, add the well whipped yolks, then the flour with baking powder and lastly the flavor. Two cupfuls of common flour with one cup of corn starch may be used instead of pastry flour.—Mrs. George Bruegger.

NO EGG CAKE.—One and one half cups of sugar, one quarter cup of butter, one cup of sour cream, two cups of chopped raisins, one teaspoon cinnamon, one half teaspoon cloves, one half teaspoon nutmeg, one tablespoon grated chocolate, one teaspoon of soda dissolved in hot water, four cups of flour. Mix spices and chocolate into flour, and add to the above, and add raisins dredged in flour. Bake one hour.—Mrs. George Bruegger.

MAHOGANY CAKE.—One half cupful chocolate cooked in one half cup of sweet milk, one and one half cups of sugar, one half cup of butter, two and one half cups of flour, one half cup sweet milk, three eggs, level teaspoon of soda, dissolved in milk. Bake in layers.—Mrs. Wolpert.

SWEET CREAM CAKE.—One large egg, beaten very light, one cup sugar beaten with egg till light as cream, one cup thick, sweet cream, one half spoon salt, one and one half cups flour, one teaspoonful baking powder.

Flavor with lemon. Beat continuously while mixing. Bake either in layers or as a loaf cake.—M. E. Cooper.

SILVER OR GOLD CAKE.—Three fourths cup butter, one and one half cups sugar, one half cup cold water, with one half teaspoon of soda dissolved in it, two and one half large cups of flour sifted with one level teaspoon of cream of tartar (or use two level teaspoons of baking powder and omit the soda and cream of tartar) and lastly the flavoring and stiffly beaten whites of eight eggs. Cream butter and sugar until light and smooth, add water but do not stir, then beat in the flour and beat five minutes. Cut in the whites and bake in a greased funnel loaf cake tin in a moderate oven forty minutes or until done when tested with a broom straw. For gold cake add the beaten yolks of eight eggs to the creamed butter and sugar and omit the whites and use scant measure of flour. Ice the gold cake with white boiled frosting.—Mrs. Whitehead.

CORN STARCH CAKE.—Two cups sugar, one cup butter, one cup of sweet milk, two cups flour, one cup corn starch, whites of seven eggs, one and one half teaspoons of baking powder. Flavor.—Contributed.

JELLY ROLL.—One cup sugar, three eggs well beaten, one cup flour, one teaspoon baking powder, one half cup boiling water added last, one half teaspoon lemon or vanilla, pinch of salt. Spread in well buttered dripping pans. When done turn out, spread with jelly and roll quickly. Makes two rolls.—Contributed.

BREAD CAKE.—Three cups bread sponge, one cup lard or butter, one pound raisins, two cups sugar, two eggs, one teaspoon soda in a little water, nutmeg and spices. Mix, raise until light and bake in one loaf.

MOCHA CAKE.—Bake a sponge cake mixture in two round layer cake pans and spread smoothly between the layers and on the outside with Mocha cream. Wash one half cup of butter, then beat to a cream and add slowly enough thick syrup to sweeten. Make syrup as follows: Cook together one cup of sugar and one half cup of clear, strong coffee until a thick syrup is formed; cool before using. (New and delicious.)

MOCHA ICING.—One quarter pound chopped almonds, blanched, put in oven to dry, one half cup of butter, eight tablespoons of icing sugar, one tablespoon of brandy or whisky; mix butter and sugar to a paste, then add almonds and whisky.

PARIS STICKS.—Three cupfuls of chopped almonds, two and one half cupfuls of pulverized sugar, the whites of five eggs beaten to a stiff froth, the grated rind of two lemons. Mix the ingredients and roll out on pulverized sugar, cut into strips an inch wide and put into paraffined pans. Bake in a slow oven. Excellent.

SUNSHINE CAKE.—Whites of seven eggs, yolks of five eggs, one third teaspoon cream of tartar, one cup sugar, one cup of flour, a little salt and vanilla. Beat whites stiff, add salt and cream of tartar, add sugar, then beaten yolks, then flour which has been sifted several times. Flavor and bake in a funnel tin.—Contributed.

MOCK ANGEL FOOD.—One cup sweet milk, bring to boiling point, one cup flour, one cup sugar, three teaspoons of baking powder. Sift dry ingredients together four times, add warm milk and stir well then fold in beaten whites of two eggs. Flavor. Bake in angel cake tins.—Contributed.

ANGEL CAKE.—Whites of twelve eggs—or, measured, one and one quarter cups of whites of eggs. Add one third of a teaspoonful of salt, and beat until stiff. Sift into this 1¼ cups of granulated sugar, and beat. Have at hand one cup of flour that you have sifted five times; sift this in and mix one teaspoonful of extract of bitter almonds, or any preferred flavor. Bake in slow oven, and do not grease your pan. With a gas stove one young friend puts the grate in the oven in its lowest sliding place and bakes her angel cake there, lighting both burners for one minute. Then she turns the front out and the other so low that it looks like a row of blue beads. She bakes it one hour. Another, equally successful, puts her grate a little higher than the middle of the oven, and bakes the cake there for one half hour with a very moderate oven.

MOCHA CAKE.—One cupful of sugar, one cupful of flour and one teaspoon of cream of tartar and one half teaspoon of soda sifted all together twice, blend in one large teaspoon of melted butter and break in the eggs and stir well, then add one half cup of boiling milk. Bake in one loaf in a moderate oven.

MOCHA FILLING.—One cupful of powdered sugar, a small piece of butter, two tablespoons of coffee, two teaspoons of vanilla. Cream butter and sugar, add coffee and flavoring gradually and a little more sugar if necessary. Spread with a knife dipped in hot water.—Contributed.

MARSHMALLOW FILLING.—One cupful of brown sugar, one cupful of white sugar, one cupful water and one tablespoon of vinegar boiled together like candy. Beat two eggs very light and stir into the candy with one quarter pound of marshmallows, cut up. Spread on layers of cake.—Contributed.

DEVIL'S FOOD.—Two eggs, one cup sugar, one half cup butter, two thirds cup sweet milk, one teaspoon vanilla, one half cup melted chocolate, one half teaspoon soda, one teaspoon baking powder, two scant cups of flour.—Mrs. Creaser.

DEVIL'S FOOD CAKE.—One egg, one cup sugar, half cup sour milk, one tablespoon butter, one fourth cup boiling water, 1 teaspoon soda, one and one half squares chocolate and one cup flour. (Can use sour cream instead of milk and butter.) Cream eggs and sugar. Melt chocolate over hot water and add butter to melt it, then add eggs and sugar. Dissolve soda in water.—Mrs. G. A. McIntosh.

BOISE BROWN CAKE.—One and one half cups sugar, three fourths cup butter, four eggs, three fourths cup grated chocolate, one cup milk, one cup chopped nuts, two cups flour, two teaspoons baking powder, one teaspoon vanilla, one teaspoon cloves, one teaspoon cinnamon, one teaspoon allspice, one half teaspoon salt.—Mrs. D. E. Plier.

MASHED POTATO CAKE.—Two cups sugar, three quarters cup butter, one cup mashed potatoes, four eggs, one cup chocolate, one half cup sweet milk, one teaspoonful cloves, one teaspoonful vanilla, one cup chopped walnut, two cups flour, two teaspoons baking powder.—Mrs. F. Kleinsorge.

CHOCOLATE LOAF CAKE.—One half cake of chocolate shaved in a bowl or three fourths cup of cocoa. Pour one cup of boiling water on this mixture and let it stand while you are mixing the cake. Cream three fourths cup of butter with two cups of sugar until light. It is best to cream the butter first and add sugar gradually especially if the butter is hard and cold. Beat in yolks of two eggs, one half cup of sour milk or butter milk, one teaspoon of soda dissolved in a little water, (about two tablespoonfuls,) two cups of flour sifted, and beaten whites of two eggs. Beat well, then add the chocolate. Bake in one sheet in a dripping pan lined with greased paper. Let the cake stand in the pan. Ice with boiled frosting and when firm and cold, cover with one square of chocolate that has been melted in one teaspoon of butter in a cup placed in a pan of hot water for five minutes. Pour the chocolate over the white frosting and spread evenly with a silver knife. Cut the cake diagonally across the pan into two inch diamond shaped pieces. A cupful of floured chopped nuts may be added to the cake batter before baking, if nut loaf is liked, and sometimes I place a half English walnut in the center of the frosting on each diamond. This chocolate and white frosting is also nice with white layer cake and chopped nuts make it extra nice for a thick filling to a square two layer cake, shaking the nuts over the white frosting and then baking them with the chocolate.—Mrs. Whitehead.

SPONGE CAKE.—Beat four eggs and one cupful of granulated sugar until mixture is creamy white. Add four tablespoons of cold water and one cup of flour sifted several times with a teaspoonful of baking powder. Bake in a moderate oven. Flavor with lemon. May be baked in layers.—Mrs. H. Hanson.

SPONGE CAKE.—Six eggs, (reserve whites of two for frosting), two cups sugar. Beat (not stir) eggs and sugar until almost cream colored, two and one half cups flour, one teaspoon flavoring, and one teaspoon baking powder last, one cup boiling water, the water must be added gradually.

While adding flour and water stir instead of beating. Bake in loaf in a moderate oven thirty or forty minutes.—Mrs. C. C. Mackenroth.

HOT WATER SPONGE CAKES.—Four eggs beaten 15 minutes, two scant cups sugar, 2 cups sifted flour, 2 teaspoons baking powder, two thirds cup boiling water, flavor with lemon or vanilla. Bake in a deep square tin.—Mrs. Southard.

BOILED SPONGE CAKE.—Five eggs, one cup white sugar, one cup flour, juice of one half lemon, one teaspoon vanilla. Boil the sugar with three tablespoons water until it threads. Pour over the stiffly beaten whites of eggs, beat this fifteen minutes, then add egg yolks, flavoring and the flour sifted three times. Bake in angel food tin.—Mrs. Aaron J. Bessie.

GOLD SPONGE CAKE.—Whites of eleven eggs beaten very stiff, yolks of four eggs beaten very light with one and one half cups of powdered sugar. Cut in the whites and add one cup of swans down flour sifted with one teaspoonful of baking powder. Flavor. Cut flour in lightly as you would for sponge cake. Bake in one loaf.—Mrs. C. H. McKay.

SNOW SPONGE CAKE WITH COCOANUT FILLING.—Beat the whites of ten eggs very light, add one and one half cupfuls of powdered sugar and beat until the bowl can be inverted and retain the eggs. Add one teaspoon cream tartar to one cupful of flour and sift several times. Cut this into the egg mixture, flavor with almond extract and turn into square ungreased cake tins, baking in two sheets. Fill with cocoanut frosting made by boiling two cupfuls of sugar with water until it hairs from the spoon, turn it hot on to the beaten whites of two eggs and whip to a frosting. Add one small cocoanut which has been freed from the shell and all brown skin and grated fine. Flavor with lemon or vanilla. If fresh cocoanut cannot be obtained try soaking the shredded cocoanut in warm milk and steaming it an hour or two before using and then squeeze it dry. This will make it more moist. If you have only one angel cake tin, split the cake through the center after it is cold and put the icing between the layers. Swans down flour is best for this cake and the fresh cocoanut make a delicious filling.—Mrs. B. G. Whitehead.

SUNSHINE CAKE.—Whites of ten eggs, yolks of six, one level teaspoonful of cream of tartar, one and one half cupfuls of sugar, sifted, one cupful of flour, sifted twice, the grated peel of one orange or one teaspoonful of lemon or vanilla or one half teaspoon of almond extract. Beat whites very stiff, then beat in one half of the sugar, beat yolks light about ten minutes, add the flavoring and balance of the sugar and beat five minutes. Mix yolks and whites lightly together and cut in the flour that has been sifted with the cream of tartar. Bake in an ungreased, funnel angel cake tin about an hour in a slow oven or 45 minutes in a moderate oven. Avoid baking too long as it makes the cake dry and coarse. When the cake shrinks from the tin at sides of the pan it is sufficiently baked. Invert the tin and let it stand until cold. If it sticks then run a knife around the edge of cake, pat the tin slightly on the bottom and sides until it drops from the pan. If a frosted cake is preferred ice it with white boiled icing.—Mrs. Whitehead.

MOCHA CAKE.—One cup sugar, one half cup butter, three quarters cup milk, two cups flour, two teaspoons baking powder, one spoon vanilla, three eggs beaten separately. Bake in small dripping pan. When cold cut into small squares. Put into oven to brown. Three cups shelled peanuts, pour over three teaspoons melted butter. When slightly browned put through meat grinder. Whip one half pound butter with two cups powdered sugar to a cream. Butter each piece of cake with this cream paste and roll into ground nuts.—Mrs. A. McKay.

NUT LOAF CAKE.—One cup sugar, one half cup butter, one half cup sweet milk, one and one half cups sifted flour, one cup chopped walnuts or hickory nuts, two eggs, two teaspoons baking powder.—Mrs. Schollander.

BLITZ KUCHEN.—One cup sugar, three fourths cup butter, four eggs, one cup of flour, one half teaspoon baking powder, grated rind and juice of one lemon. Cream butter and sugar and then add eggs, one at a time and stirring each five minutes, then add the flour and spread dough in square tin about half an inch thick. Chop one fourth pound almonds, mix with sugar and cinnamon and sprinkle on top of cake before putting in the oven. Bake about thirty minutes.—Mrs. J. Bruegger. German Cookery.

SOUR CREAM NUT CAKE.—Break two eggs into a large cup and fill with sour cream. Put in a mixing bowl and add a level teaspoonful of soda and one cupful of sugar, beat all well add flour to make quite stiff and flavor with vanilla. Take a pound of English walnuts, chop all but what you wish to put on top of cake and stir into the batter. Bake in moderate oven. Ice the tops and lay on the half meats.—Mrs. G. A. McIntosh.

DARK CAKE.—One cup sugar, one cup butter and lard mixed, three eggs, one half cup black molasses, one cup cold coffee, one level teaspoon soda, two pounds raisins, flour to thicken. Bake in moderate oven.—Mrs. W. C. Lynch.

DARK COFFEE CAKE.—One cup sugar, pinch of salt, one cup shortening (butter and lard) one cup cold coffee, one cup sour cream or milk (add that ingredient), three fourths cup molasses, two level teaspoonfuls soda dissolved in warm water, cloves, cinnamon, allspice and nutmeg to suit the taste, one pound raisins, and flour enough to make a nice batter. Nuts may also be used if desired.—Mrs. W. S. Davidson.

RAISIN CAKE.—Four eggs, one cup butter, two cups brown sugar, three cups flour, one cup sour milk, one teaspoon soda, dissolved in very little water, one small teaspoon each of cinnamon, cloves and allspice, one half teaspoon vanilla. This is very nice used as a layer cake with carmel icing.—Mrs. Aaron J. Bessie.

COFFEE CAKE.—One cup sugar, one cup butter, one cup coffee, one cup molasses, one teaspoon soda, one teaspoon cinnamon, one teaspoon allspice, one half teaspoon cloves, nutmeg and lemon essence. Four cups flour, one half pound raisins.—Mrs. Mary Harvey.

FRUIT SPICE CAKE.—One scant cup butter, one cup brown sugar, one fourth cup molasses, whites of three eggs, yolks of three eggs, three fourths cup water, one fourth teaspoonful baking soda. Three cups flour, one teaspoon each of cinnamon, allspice, cloves and nutmeg, mixed. One half cup raisins, one fourth cup currants, and one fourth cup citron. Mix like any batter cake adding molasses to the butter and sugar. Remember to add soda last.—Dorothy Whitehead.

SALT PORK CAKE.—One pound of salt pork chopped fine. Pour one half pint of boiling water on it, add one cup molasses, one teaspoon of soda, two cups sugar, spices to suit taste, one pound of seeded and dredged raisins and of currants and one cup of nuts, chopped. Stir thick with flour about three and one half cups. Bake in one loaf. Cut into pieces and steamed, this cake makes delicious pudding, served with pudding sauce. It calls for no butter or eggs so is a cheap cake when these foods are scarce and high priced.—Mrs. Whitehead.

CHOCOLATE COFFEE CAKE.—One cup granulated sugar, one half scant cup of butter, yolks of two eggs and one white, one half cup strong coffee warmed on stove with two squares of Bakers chocolate, one and one half cups of flour sifted with two small teaspoons of baking powder. Cream butter and sugar, then beat in eggs. Cool coffee and chocolate and add lastly the flour, and a cup of chopped nuts. Bake in a moderate oven in one loaf or in two layers. Ice with chocolate or white icing.—Mrs. A. D. Paulson.

BREAD CAKE.—Three cups bread dough, three cups sugar, one cup of butter, three eggs, one teaspoon each cinnamon, cloves and mace, a little ginger, one cup raisins, one cup currants, one half teaspoon soda. Let rise one hour and bake.—Mrs. R. J. Walker.

COFFEE CAKE.—Two or three cups of bread sponge, one cup of sugar, two eggs well beaten, one pint of milk, (luke warm), two tablespoons of melted butter or lard, one teaspoon of lemon extract or lemon juice, one half teaspoon of nutmeg, one teaspoon salt. Mix all well and add enough flour to make a stiff batter, set aside to rise, when light take out and spread into well greased dripping pans. Spread melted butter over top then mix three tablespoons of melted butter, one cup of sugar and flour enough to make it dry and lumpy, to this add a little cinnamon then sprinkle over top quite thick and bake twenty to thirty minutes.

FIG CAKE.—One pound of powdered sugar, ten eggs, ten crackers rolled fine, one half cake of sweet chocolate grated, one half pound of figs, chopped fine, one teaspoon cinnamon, one teaspoon allspice, one teaspoon baking powder. Whip the yolks of eggs very light, add sugar, then beat again, add part of rolled cracker, then add the grated chocolate, chopped figs, spices and lastly the well beaten whites of eggs alternately with remaining crackers, into which the baking powder is mixed. Bake in medium oven one hour very quietly, being careful not to shake the stove.

RYE BREAD TORTE.—One pound powder sugar, ten eggs well beaten, three ounces of rye bread, (grated), one half cake of sweet chocolate (grated), one half cup of fine chopped sweet almonds, one half cup of citron, cut fine, one teaspoon cloves, one teaspoon baking powder. Whip the yolk of egg, add the sugar and beat again, add a portion of the bread crumbs, then add the chocolate, citron, spice and almonds, mix the baking powder in the remaining bread crumbs, lastly the well beaten whites of eggs, alternately with the bread crumbs. Bake in a medium oven about one hour. This may also be made in layers and whipped cream placed between. —Mrs. George Bruegger.

GRIES TORTE OR FARINA CAKE.—One cup farina, one cup sugar, eight eggs. Beat sugar and yolks of eggs one half hour then add farina slowly, and the well beaten whites last. Bake one hour by slow fire. When cooled put sliced pineapple on top and whipped cream.—Mrs. J. Bruegger.

FRUIT CAKE.—Cream one pound of brown sugar and one pound of butter, add one pound of eggs (beaten light) one pound of flour sifted with two teaspoons of baking powder, one nutmeg (grated) one tablespoon each of cloves and allspice, half a pint of brandy and two pounds each of seeded raisins and of currants, one half pound of chopped citron. Flour the fruit well before adding to cake mixture. Bake in one loaf in moderate oven.

Pour half a pint of wine over it while it is warm, after baking.—Mrs. George Newton.

MOTHER'S FRUIT CAKE.—One pound of butter, one and one half pounds of sugar, one pound of flour, one cupful of New Orleans molasses, one teaspoon of soda dissolved in two tablespoons of water, two teaspoons of cinnamon, one teaspoonful of cloves and one teaspoonful of mace, one dozen eggs, one gill or one cup of brandy, three pounds of raisins, (seeded), two pounds of dried currants, one pound of shredded citron, one pound stoned dates and one pound of shelled English walnuts or pecans, cream the butter and sugar until light, add beaten yolks of eggs, add the molasses, soda and spices. Clean and cut the fruit and dredge thoroughly with part of the flour, stir it into the mixture alternately with the flour and beaten whites of eggs. Mix well and lastly add the brandy. Bake in one large loaf very slowly. Test with a broom straw to be sure that the cake is well baked. The batter will seem thin but do not add extra flour if you want a rich moist fruit cake. Put in cake box and it will keep many months. Pieces of it can be quickly steamed and used with foam sauce as plum pudding for dessert in an emergency which is sometimes worth the price of the cake.—Mrs. B. G. Whitehead.

FRUIT CAKE.—Rub one pound butter and one and one half pounds sugar to a cream, add eight eggs and beat. Now add one tablespoon lemon extract, one grated nutmeg, one tablespoon cinnamon, one half teaspoon cloves, one pint sour cream. Now add four pounds raisins, one pound citron, two pounds almonds, two pounds English walnuts, two pounds flour with two teaspoons soda in it, one glass jelly. Bake three and one half hours in moderate oven. Pour one cup brandy over the top of cake after it is baked. —Mrs. Southard.

IMPERIAL FRUIT CAKE.—One pound of sugar, one pound of flour, three quarters pound of butter, one pound of almonds, blanched and cut fine, 1-2 pound of citron, 1-4 pound candied cherries and as much pineapple, one half pound of seeded raisins, rind and juice of one lemon, two pieces of candied orange, one nutmeg, ten eggs. This is very delicious and will keep

for months. No baking powder or soda are used but the eggs are beaten separately, yolks added to creamed butter and sugar and the stiff whites put in last of all. Bake in one loaf in a slow oven. Ice with white boiled frosting.
—Contributed.

BLANCHE'S DATE CAKE.—Beat three egg yolks with one cup of sugar, add one cup of flour sifted with one teaspoon of baking powder, stiffly beaten whites of three eggs and one pound of stoned dates and one pound chopped nuts, (pecans, English walnuts or hickory nuts). Bake in one loaf in a moderate oven. Remove from oven and while it is hot pour one cup of sour cream over it. The cream soaks into the cake and makes it moist like fruit cake. No butter is used in this recipe.—Mrs. Whitehead.

GINGER BREAD.—One half cup sugar, one half cup butter, one cup molasses, each one teaspoon (heaped), ginger, cloves and cinnamon, two level teaspoons soda in one cup boiling water, three scant cups of flour, two well beaten eggs. Make it in the above order. Eggs last.—Mrs. F. Kleinsorge.

GINGER BREAD.—One cup of butter, one cup of sugar, one cup of molasses, (New Orleans), one cup of boiling water, two eggs beaten in batter one at a time, one teaspoon of soda dissolved in the water, two and one half cups of flour, two tablespoons of ginger, one teaspoon of nutmeg. Bake in a loaf or in gem tins.—Mrs. John Heffernan.

GOOD PLAIN GINGER BREAD—One cup of molasses, one cup of sugar, one cup of boiling water, two level teaspoons of soda dissolved in the hot water, one half cupful (generous) of butter or shortening, one large teaspoon of ginger and a little salt. Add enough flour to make pretty stiff, about three cups. Bake in moderate oven in one sheet. As molasses cake of any kind burns easily care should be taken not to have the oven too hot. Eat warm for luncheon. Is nice sliced cold and served with whipped cream as a dessert also.—Mrs. Whitehead.

WALNUT FILLING FOR CAKE.—One pound chopped walnut meats, yolks of six eggs, two cups sugar, one cup sour cream, flavor with vanilla.

Boil in double boiler until thick and beat until cool. Spread between layers of cake.—Mrs. Aaron J. Bessie.

RAISIN FILLING FOR CAKE.—One tablespoon of butter, two tablespoons of flour, four tablespoons of sugar. Mix well together, add enough hot water to cream it. Cook in double boiler until thick. Remove from fire and add one half package of raisins and two tablespoons of frosting.—Mrs. John Heffernan.

BOILED FROSTING.—Two cups of sugar boiled with water till it threads from spoon. Beat whites of two eggs very stiff. Pour the thick hot syrup gradually into the whites, beating continually until light and thick. Flavor to suit taste. For chocolate frosting add one third cake of Bakers chocolate cut or shaved fine, while the frosting is warm enough to melt it. For tutti-fruitti filling add mixed chopped nuts, raisins, figs, dates or crystalized fruits to two thirds of the frosting, reserving the balance for icing the top of cake. For cocoanut cake, spread the layers with frosting and sprinkle thickly with grated cocoanut. Marsh mallows may be steamed, mixed with nuts, and served through the frosting too.—Mrs. Whitehead.

WHITE CARAMEL OR FONDANT FROSTING.—Two cups of sugar, boiled with one and three fourths cups of milk or thin cream to the soft ball stage. Test it by dropping a spoonful in cold water. If you can pick it up in a soft ball take the carmel from the stove. Add one tablespoon of (uncolored) butter and one teaspoon of vanilla and beat steadily until it creams or turns to a fondant. Spread immediately on the cake. Chopped nuts are nice added to this or halved English walnuts may be placed regularly on top of a square cake. Chocolate may be added to the warm fondant before beating it. White icing like this is nice covered with thin layer of chocolate melted with butter or English walnuts buried in the white icing and then covered with chocolate fondant makes a delicious filling for layer cake. This caramel filling with nuts is especially nice on Devil's Food or dark chocolate. Brown sugar caramel is made likewise using half granulated and half brown sugar for the fondant.—Mrs. Whitehead.

Cookies, Drop Cakes and Doughnuts

"Bake, bake, bake! For the cookie jar piled high
But yesterday, in some curious way,
Is empty again, O my!
Stir, stir, stir, in the froth of yellow and white
For well she knows how the story goes
Of a small boy's appetite."—J. W. Foley.

GERMAN CHRISTMAS COOKIES.—There are many different kinds and I will give you the names of them just as they are called in German as some names cannot be well translated into English language. The first will be Springelie. One pound of sugar, one pound of flour, four eggs, butter the size of a walnut and one half teaspoon of baking powder. Beat sugar and butter, and eggs one at a time, beating for fifteen minutes, then add flour with baking powder, now roll and cut, sprinkle baking board with flour and anise seeds, and lay cookies on that until next morning, then bake in a moderate oven a light yellow.

WEISSE PFEFFER NUSSE.—One pound of flour, one pound of sugar, four large eggs, three ounces of citron, the grated rind of one lemon, one nutmeg, one tablespoon cinnamon, one teaspoonful of cloves, one teaspoon of baking powder. Eggs, sugar, baking powder and spices must be well beaten, then mix with flour and citron; roll and cut and let lay over night or form into little balls and bake until they become dry inside.

EIER KRANZE.—One pound of flour, one pound of butter, one fourth pound of sugar, the yolks of six hard boiled eggs, one half cupful of brandy. Rub the boiled yolks and mix with the flour and butter, (which have been rubbed smooth together like pie crust) then sugar is added and the grated yolks of hard boiled eggs; then add brandy. Roll and cut with doughnut cutter, brush with beaten egg and sprinkle with sugar, cinnamon and chopped almond. Bake in hot oven.

BAISORS OR KISSES.—Beat the whites of six eggs and three cups of sugar one hour or until the egg beater will stand in the mixture without falling, then flavor with vanilla and drop by spoonful on a tin and bake in a moderate oven.—Mrs. John Bruegger demonstrated all of the above recipes in the German Cookery series for the club meeting of June 9, 1909.

COOKIES.—Take two quarts of flour and two cups of sugar, sift the two together, then add one heaping cup of lard or butter; rub well through the flour and sugar and then add four teaspoons of baking powder and rub well through the flour, sugar and butter. Then make a hole in the center and into it break five eggs and a half cup of sweet milk and flavor to taste. Stir these contents together, roll out and bake in hot oven.—Mrs. F. Kleinsorge.

MRS. HAYES' DATE COOKIES.—One cup butter, one half cup lard, one and one half cups brown sugar, one half cup sour milk, one teaspoon soda, three cups oat meal, two cups flour, mix, one pound dates, one cup sugar, one cup water, boil one hour till it is a smooth paste. Roll the dough as thin as you can and cut with a small round cutter. Place one teaspoon of date paste on a cooky, then cover with another. Bake in a moderate oven.—Mrs. Creaser.

ROSETTES.—Two eggs, one teaspoonful of sugar, one fourth teaspoonful salt, one cup of milk, one cup of flour, (a little more if necessary). Mix flour and milk smooth then add sugar and salt and the beaten eggs. Heat the rosette iron in the hot lard then dip into batter, not letting batter come over the top of iron, now return to the hot lard covering the iron with same for at least twenty five seconds. Drain and sprinkle with powdered sugar and serve as cakes.—Mrs. J. Bruegger.

MARGUERITES.—One cup sugar, one third cup water. Boil until it threads or hairs and beat into beaten white of eggs. Add nuts and spread on

Saratoga flakes and brown in oven.—Mrs. G. A. McIntosh.

OAT MEAL COOKIES WITH DATE FILLING.—One cup light brown sugar, one and one half cups butter, one half cup sour milk, three cups oat meal, two cups flour, one teaspoon soda in milk.

DATE FILLING.—One pound dates chopped, one cup sugar, one cup boiling water, cook until thick. Spread between cookies. Press together on edges and bake.—Mrs. G. A. McIntosh.

OAT MEAL COOKIES.—One cup butter, one cup sugar, two eggs, six tablespoons sweet milk, three fourths teaspoon soda, one half teaspoon each of cinnamon, cloves and nutmeg, one cup chopped raisins, one half cup currants, two cups flour, two cups oat meal, three fourths cup chopped walnuts. Drop from teaspoon into greased pan and bake.—Contributed.

OAT MEAL COOKIES, DATE FILLING.—Four cups of oat meal, two cups of flour, one cup of shortening, three quarters cup of sugar, one teaspoon of soda, water to roll. Roll thin, bake and put two together with cooked dates.—Mrs. Geo. Farries.

OAT MEAL DROP COOKIES.—Three quarters cup butter, one cup sugar, cream together, three eggs well beaten, two cups flour, two cups of rolled oats, one and one half cups seeded chopped raisins, one teaspoon cinnamon, three quarters teaspoon soda. Drop on buttered tins and bake in slow oven. —Mrs. Geo. Farries.

GOOD COOKIES.—One and a half cups sugar, three fourths cup butter. Rub butter and sugar to a cream, (three eggs) beating them into the cream one at a time, three tablespoons of cream, or sweet milk, one teaspoon cream tartar, half teaspoon soda, (soda dissolved in milk, cream of tartar put through sieve with flour), flour enough to roll thin, flavor with teaspoon nutmeg and vanilla. Sprinkle with sugar and cut out. Bake in a hot oven.— Mrs. John Heffernan.

CHOCOLATE COOKIES.—One tablespoon lard, one half cup butter, one cup sugar, pinch of salt, one half teaspoon cinnamon, one half teaspoon soda, dissolve in very little cold milk, two ounces melted chocolate, two cups flour. Roll very thin, cut and bake in greased tins.—Mrs. Aaron J. Bessie.

EGGLESS COOKIES.—Two cups sugar, one cup sweet milk, one cup butter, one half teaspoon soda, (dissolved in cold water), lemon extract, flour enough to roll out.—Mrs. Aaron J. Bessie.

OAT MEAL COOKIES.—One cup butter, one and one third cups sugar, two eggs, one and three fourths cup raw oat meal, two cups flour, three fourths teaspoon of soda, one half teaspoon salt, one teaspoonful cinnamon, one and one half cups raisins, and three fourths cup of sour milk. Drop by teaspoonful into floured tins and bake in a very moderate oven.—Clara Cooper.

ALMOND RINGS.—Three fourths pound of butter creamed with one half pound powdered sugar; add three yolks of eggs (beaten) and one pound of flour. Flavor with vanilla or almond extract. Mix and roll thin. Cut in large rings. Beat three whites of eggs to a froth, brush over the cookies and sprinkle thickly with chopped almond, granulated sugar and cinnamon. Brown in the oven.—Mrs. Whitehead.

CHOCOLATE NUT KISSES.—Ten ounces of powdered sugar beaten with the whites of six eggs for one hour. Add ten ounces of grated chocolate and seven ounces of ground almond. Bake like kisses in a moderate oven.—Mrs. Whitehead.

COCOANUT DROP CAKES.—Two cupfuls of sugar boiled with one cupful of water until it threads from the spoon. Beat the whites of two eggs very light. Beat in the hot syrup and beat until light and thick, flavor with vanilla or lemon and stir very stiff with shredded cocoanut. Drop in little stiff cakes on buttered papers on tins and brown a delicate color in a moderate oven. Invert the papers and brush the backs of paper with a little cold water when the cakes will readily slip off. Chopped pecans may be used instead of cocoanut but there must be enough nuts to make a stiff mixture that will not run when dropped on the papers.—Mrs. Whitehead.

ROCKS.—Two cups brown sugar, one cup butter, one cup cold strong coffee, two eggs, one level teaspoon soda, one teaspoon baking powder, sifted with three cups flour, one teaspoon cinnamon, one teaspoon nutmeg, two cups seeded raisins, one cup nuts chopped but not fine. Roll out and cut into cookies. Bake in quick oven. Very good.—Mrs. Alta Southard.

VANILLA WAFERS OR CRISP COOKIES.—One half cup of lard and butter mixed. Cream with one cup of sugar; add one well beaten egg, one fourth cup of milk, two and one half cups of flour, one teaspoon baking powder, one half teaspoon of salt and two teaspoons of vanilla. Mix soft in order given, flour board and roll very thin. Cut into small cookies and bake in a hot oven.—Mrs. Whitehead.

SUGAR COOKIES.—One half cup butter creamed with one cup sugar, add two beaten eggs, one fourth cup milk, two and one half cups flour, one large teaspoon baking powder, one half teaspoon of lemon extract and grated nutmeg if liked. Mix soft and roll but sprinkle with sugar, roll it in then cut and bake in greased pans in a hot oven.—Contributed.

BROWN COOKIES.—Mix two cups of brown sugar with one cup of lard, add one cup of cooking molasses, and one cup of boiling water with two teaspoons of soda dissolved in it, one tablespoon of ginger. Mix in flour enough to make a stiff dough and let it stand over night. Roll out quite thick, cut and bake. When cool spread with a stiff icing of lemon juice and powdered sugar.—Mrs. Harry Hanson.

MOTHER'S WHITE COOKIES.—Two eggs, one cup of sugar, one cupful of butter, one half cupful of sour milk, one half teaspoon of soda, nutmeg to taste, one teaspoonful of baking powder. Flour enough to make soft dough. Roll thin and bake.—Mrs. E. G. Schollander.

GINGER SNAPS.—Heat to boiling point one cup butter, add one cup molasses, two cups brown sugar, one tablespoon ginger, one tablespoon cinnamon, one scant teaspoon soda. Take from fire, beat well, add two eggs. Roll with six cups of flour. Let stand over night.—Mrs. E. Schollander.

CLARA'S DROP CAKES.—Two cups sugar, two eggs, one cup sweet milk, one teaspoon soda, one teaspoon cinnamon, one cup raisins, one cup shortening, one cup molasses, four cups flour, one teaspoon salt, one teaspoon cloves, one cup currants. Mix together sugar and shortening, stir in eggs beaten lightly, add soda dissolved in molasses, cloves, cinnamon, milk, fruit, mixed with a little of the flour and lastly the flour and salt sifted together. Drop from teaspoon on greased tin and bake in moderate oven. This makes quite a large amount.—Clara Monroe.

PEPPER GINGER COOKIES.—One cup sugar, one cup molasses, one cup shortening (mixed lard and butter, one tablespoon ginger, 1 fourth teaspoon (scant) black pepper, one teaspoon soda in one cup boiling water. Mix with flour enough to roll out, about three large cups. Roll thin, cut into cookies and bake in greased tins in a moderate oven. Cheap and good.—Contributed.

OAT MEAL COOKIES WITH DATE FILLING.—One cup of sugar, one cup butter, creamed together, add two eggs, beat and then add one half of a large cup of sour milk with one teaspoon soda dissolved in it, two cups of raw rolled oats and two cups of flour, a little salt. Flavor with vanilla or lemon and roll and cut into small cookies. Chopped raisins may be mixed with the dough or a date filling may be used, made as follows: Boil one pound of stoned dates with one cup of water and one cup of sugar to a thick paste. Spread a teaspoon of Dates on each cookie, cover with another cookie, press edges together firmly and bake in moderate oven.—Mrs. Whitehead.

SOFT MOLASSES COOKIES.—Two cups molasses boiled, one cup lard and butter put into boiling molasses, two eggs or yolks of four or five, two cups sugar, one cup sour milk, one half teaspoon nutmeg, one half teaspoon cloves, one heaping teaspoon each of ginger and cinnamon, pinch of salt, two heaping teaspoons soda, flour to roll very soft. Do not let molasses boil more than a minute or two.—Mrs. Paul Leonhardy.

HERMITS.—One and one half cups brown sugar, one cup butter, one half teaspoon soda, three eggs, pinch of salt, nutmeg, one and one half cups chopped raisins or dates, one and one half cups chopped nuts, three and one half cups flour, one teaspoonful of cream of tartar. Drop these in small, stiff, rough cakes on greased tins and bake brown. For chocolate hermits, add one half cup of grated Bakers chocolate before baking or shave the chocolate and melt it in a little hot water. Cocoa may be substituted for chocolate.—Contributed.

FATTIGMAND. (Scandinavian).—Three well beaten eggs, three tablespoons of sugar, three teaspoons of cream, add cardamom seeds to flavor and one teaspoon of brandy. Stir well together, add flour to roll soft, roll, cut in fancy strips or small cookies and fry in hot lard like crullers.—Contributed.

BERLINER KRARZE. (Scandinavian). Four raw egg yolks, three hard boiled egg yolks (grated), one cup sugar, one cup butter, three and one half cups of flour. Flavor with one tablespoon of brandy or with any favorite extract. Roll thin, cut, dip cookies into beaten whites of eggs, then into rolled loaf sugar and bake or finely chopped nuts and cinnamon may be sprinkled on them just before baking.—Contributed.

"S" FINGERS. (Scandinavian).—One cup sugar, one half cup butter, two eggs, four tablespoons of milk, two teaspoons of baking powder. Flour to roll stiff and flavoring. Roll thin, cut into letter "S" fingers and bake in greased pans.

JUMBLES.—One cup sugar, one cup molasses, three eggs, one cup sour cream mixed with two level teaspoons of soda. Add four cups flour, one half teaspoon ginger, one fourth teaspoon cloves and a little salt. Drop in small cakes on greased pans and bake in moderate oven.—Contributed.

> "Cook says it's awful 'scouragin' to bake and fret and fuss,
> An' w'en she thinks she's got 'em in the crock they're all in us!"—J. W. Foley.

DOUGHNUTS.—One and one half cups sugar, three eggs, one cup sour cream, one half cup milk sweet or sour, one half teaspoon soda dissolved in water and stirred into the cream, two teaspoons baking powder with flour to make soft dough, season to taste.—Mrs. L. L. Lampman.

DOUGHNUTS.—Three eggs beaten light, one cup sugar, two tablespoons butter, one cup sour milk, one teaspoon soda dissolved in hot water, one half teaspoon nutmeg, a little salt, one half teaspoon baking powder. Use swansdown cake flour to make a nice smooth dough. Roll, cut and fry brown in deep smoking hot lard.—Mrs. Southard.

DOUGHNUTS.—Two cups sugar, two eggs, one cup sweet milk, one heaping teaspoon butter, one and one half cups mashed potatoes, salt, nutmeg, three teaspoons baking powder. Mash the potatoes and while they are hot add the butter, sugar, salt and nutmeg. Beat the eggs and add with the milk, sift baking powder with flour twice. Use only flour to roll out, the less flour used the better doughnuts will be.—Mrs. Aaron J. Bessie.

SOUR CREAM DOUGHNUTS.—One and one half cups sour milk, one half cup thick sour cream, one level teaspoon of soda, one and one half cups sugar, three eggs, a little salt and nutmeg or other flavoring. Flour to roll soft, about six cups, cut. Brown in deep, smoking hot fat, drain and sift powdered sugar over them, (two eggs will do).—Contributed.

EXTRA GOOD DOUGHNUTS.—One cup sugar, one cup sweet milk, one half (scant) cup sour cream, three eggs, two level teaspoons baking powder, one level teaspoon soda, salt. Flour to roll soft. Pour sweet milk over sugar, add soda to cream, stir in milk and sugar, then eggs and then flour, flavoring, etc.—Contributed.

Pastry, Pies and Tarts

"Cook your husband what he likes, and save a hundred household strikes."

PIE CRUST.—For one pie, mix one large cup of flour sifted with half a teaspoon of salt, with one half cup of lard and butter mixed. Blend these ingredients thoroughly with the hands or cut and shape with a knife, then lightly mix in one quarter cup ice cold water, just enough to bind the flour and lard together. Use scant measure of water and do not handle much. Flour the molding board and quickly roll half the dough into a thin crust and line the pie tin. Fill the pie with prepared fruit, wet the edges of the crust with water, roll out the balance of the dough for the upper crust, gash it across the center and lift it carefully and cover the pie, pressing edges together with a fork. If a glazed crust is wanted rub the crust over with a little milk, egg and sugar slightly mixed together. This insures a nice brown crust. The oven should be hot enough to turn white note paper a nice, rich brown color in five minutes time. Pastry requires a brisk oven but not too hot. The ingredients for pastry should be very cold. The measure of shortening (lard) should be generous and the water scant and it should not be handled after the water is added only sufficient to lift out of the mixing bowl and roll out. Flour the board well and flour the rolling pin.

CURRANT PIE.—One cup currants (fresh fruit), one cup sugar, one tablespoon flour, two tablespoons water, one lump of butter and yolks of two eggs. Beat all together and bake in one crust. When done frost with the beaten whites of the eggs.—Mrs. Davidson.

CHERRY PIE.—Line a pie plate with pie crust, fill it generously half full of fresh, stoned sour cherries, and sprinkle a generous cupful of sugar over them mixed with one large tablespoon of flour, dot with one level tablespoon of butter cut into bits, cover with another layer of cherries sprinkled lightly with sugar. Cover with an upper crust wetting the edges and pressing well together to prevent juice escaping. Cut a gash in center of top crust to allow steam to escape and bake in a moderate oven for forty minutes or until cherries are tender and the juice bubbles in a simp. If a novice at the work, test the fruit with a broom straw through the gash in the upper crust. If the straw can pierce the fruit easily the pie is done.—Mrs. Whitehead.

FRESH FRUIT PIES.—The recipe for cherry pie applies to all fresh berry or fruit pies gauging the sugar and flour according to the juicy sweetness of the fruit. Gooseberries, currants, strawberries, cranberries and plums will take good full measures of sugar and flour. Raspberries, blue berries and black berries require less sugar and apricots and peaches and apples small measures of flour. A little butter improves the flavor of all fruit pies and apple pie needs a dusting of nutmeg or cinnamon before adding the top crust. Canned fruit may be drained free of its syrup and used the same way using less sugar and adding half a cupful of the syrup.—L. W. W.

LEMON PIE. Crust.—One half large cup of flour, one heaping tablespoon of lard, pinch of salt. Mix well. Add enough water to make paste. Roll thin, put in tin, prick with fork and bake. Filling. One large cup of sugar, two heaping tablespoons of flour, one large cup of boiling water, butter the size of a walnut, juice and grated rind of one lemon, yolks of two eggs. Mix the flour and sugar together, add boiling water, put on the stove and let come to a boil, then add butter, yolks of two eggs, juice and grated rind of one lemon. Remove from fire at once. Beat the whites of two eggs with two tablespoons of sugar and put on top. Put in oven to brown.—Mrs. R. Meidell.

AMERICAN PRUNE PIE.—Stew about twenty four or thirty prunes, pitt and sweeten the prunes. Bake a pie crust. Whip one half pint of cream, sweeten with sugar, flavor with vanilla. Put a layer of prunes in the crust, then the whipped cream on top and serve cold.—Mrs. R. Meidell.

PUMPKIN PIE.—One cupful of mashed pumpkin, three quarters cup of sugar, one teaspoonful of salt, one half teaspoonful each of mace, cinnamon and ginger. Heat one teacupful of milk and beat three eggs and add to mixture. Bake with under crust only.—Mrs. H. Hanson.

PUMPKIN PIE.—One quart milk, three cups stewed pumpkin, one tablespoon flour, four eggs, one and one half cups brown sugar, one half cup molasses, one teaspoon salt, one level tablespoon cinnamon, one teaspoon ginger, one tablespoon melted butter. Bake with an under crust. Makes three pies. Beat eggs, add pumpkin, then flour, sugar, salt, spices, molasses and butter and lastly the milk which may be partly cream. Mix well, fill pie tins which have been lined with pie crust and bake from thirty to forty minutes.—L. W. W.

RHUBARB PIE.—One cup diced fresh rhubarb, one cup sugar, one tablespoon flour. Mix all together, turn into a pie tin lined with pie crust. Dot bits of butter over the top of rhubarb, sprinkle with one tablespoon of water. Cover with top crust and bake in moderate oven about forty minutes. —Contributed.

CREAM PIE.—Two yolks of eggs beaten with one half cup sugar, add one large tablespoon of flour and a scant tablespoon of corn starch dissolved in a little milk. Cook in one pint of boiling milk on back of range, stirring constantly. Flavor with vanilla or lemon. Fill baked pastry shell, cover with meringue and brown in oven. Serve cold.—L. W. W.

CUSTARD PIES.—The rule for custard pie is four beaten eggs and one scant cup sugar to each quart of milk. For one small pie use half this recipe. Mix all together and add flavoring of vanilla, lemon, almond or nutmeg. Line deep pie tin with pie crust and fill with the raw custard and bake in a moderate oven until the custard sets and can be cut clean with a silver knife. Do not bake too long or it will be dry and tough and use scant sugar measure to avoid a watery custard. Cocoanut custard pie is made by adding one cup of shredded cocoanut before baking. Date pie is made by pressing stewed dates through a colander and adding to the custard. Open fruit custard pies are made by laying a layer of prepared fruit on the crust in the tin and covering with the raw custard. All custard pies are baked with an under crust only. Pumpkin, squash and sweet potato pies are made by adding a quart of the cooked and mashed vegetable to each quart of custard and adding spices and salt to suit individual taste.—Contributed.

CREAM PIES.—The cream fillings are cooked on top of stove until thick. Line pie tins with a rich pie crust, pick with a fork to let out air while baking, and bake a golden brown, then fill with the cooked filling, cover with a meringue and bake until meringue sets. The rule for the cream filling is two eggs beaten with half a cup of sugar and one large tablespoon of flour or one scant tablespoon of cornstarch mixed smooth with a little milk, add flavoring. Bring two small cups of milk or water to a boil, add the egg mixture and cook thick. If liked add one teaspoon of butter to the milk or water. For chocolate pie double the sugar and use two squares of chocolate shaved fine and heat with the cream filling. For pineapple add grated pineapple to the cream filling, double the measure of flour as acids thin the mixture considerably. For lemon cream pie use the juice and grated rind of one large lemon or two small ones and double the flour and sugar measure. (For orange pie use juice of one large orange and half a lemon.) In lemon and orange pie water is generally used in preference to milk and if a rich pie is liked use an extra egg yolk and a large measure of sugar.—Contributed.

MERINGUE.—To make the meringue, beat the whites of two eggs very light and stiff, cut in two level tablespoons of sugar and beat five minutes. Spread on top of the filled pie, sprinkle lightly with sugar and brown in a slow oven. When meringue is firm to the touch it is done and will not fall or shrink, if under-done it falls. If the oven is too hot leave the oven door open for three minutes before putting the meringue in to bake. Long beating of the whites of eggs and sugar however will usually make a good, thick and firm meringue.—Contributed.

ENGLISH ORANGE CHEESE CAKES OR TARTS.—One half pound sugar (one cup) mixed with one fourth pound butter (one half cup) add three eggs, (reserving white of one); juice of two oranges and grated rind of one;

juice of one lemon. Beat well. Simmer until like honey. Fill baked patty or tart shells of pie crust. Make a meringue of the stiffly beaten white of egg and one tablespoon of sugar. Frost the tarts, sprinkle with sugar and brown in a moderate oven. Serve cold.—Mrs. Whitehead.

DEVIL'S FOOD CAKE.—One and one half cups of sugar, creamed with one half cup butter, yolks of three eggs, one half cup milk, one square chocolate melted in half cup boiling water, two cups flour sifted with two heaping teaspoons baking powder. Add vanilla and the unbeaten whites of the three eggs the last thing.—Mrs. T. B. Huff.

BURNT SUGAR CAKE.—One and one half cups sugar creamed with one half cup butter, yolks of three eggs, one large cup cold water, three large tablespoons of thick burnt sugar or enough to make a light brown in color; two cups flour sifted with two heaping teaspoons baking powder. Add the unbeaten whites of the three eggs and vanilla the last thing. Frost with boiled frosting to which has been added one tablespoon of burnt sugar and a half cup broken nut meats.—Mrs. T. B. Huff.

TO MAKE BURNT SUGAR.—Put in a sauce pan one cup sugar and cook, stirring constantly; the sugar will then form into lumps, then melt and throw off a thick black smoke. Now take from fire and add three tablespoons hot water and place on stove and let come to a good boil; it is then ready to use and can be kept indefinitely.—Mrs. T. B. Huff.

CHOCOLATE FROSTING.—To make a good chocolate frosting make a quantity of fudge, beating it until very smooth and until it sets. Then add a teaspoon, or the necessary amount of cream, or milk, until the right consistency to spread.—Mrs. T. B. Huff.

BAKED FISH.—Large white fish, pike or cat fish are best, but small fish can also be used. Put in a pan, sprinkle well with salt and pepper and cover with bits of butter; then pour a little water or milk in the pan and bake, basting the fish often, and adding more water or milk as needed. This takes about a half hour to bake in a hot oven. Make a white gravy of milk, butter and flour, season well and add a can of mushroom and serve over the fish. Delicious.—Mrs. T. B. Huff.

COCOANUT CHEESE CAKES OR TARTS.—Boil one pint of sugar with two thirds of a pint of water and add one and one half cups of shredded cocoanut and boil slowly twelve minutes; remove to rear of range and while warm beat in one half cup of butter until smooth; then beat in the beaten yolks of five or six eggs. Flavor with lemon juice or vanilla or almond extract. Line patty pans or gem tins with a rich pastry crust, fill with the cocoanut custard and bake. They are pretty capped with a cube of currant jelly. Serve either hot or cold.

APPLE CHEESE CAKES.—One pint of steamed, sweetened and stewed apple sauce heated. Add grated rind of half a lemon, two level tablespoons of butter and beat smooth, then cut in two eggs beaten well. Bake in patty pans lined with pastry. Good way to use left over pie crust and apple sauce.

MINCE MEAT.—Four pounds of lean boiled meat, chopped fine; twice its weight in sour apples, peeled, cored and chopped fine, one pound of minced suet; three pounds of seeded raisins, two pounds of currants; one pound of brown sugar; one pint of molasses and of maple syrup or of fruit syrup, two quarts of sweet fresh cider, one pint of cider boiled, one tablespoon of salt, one scant teaspoon of pepper, one tablespoon each of mace, allspice and cloves, four tablespoons of cinnamon. Mix well and bring to a boil on the stove. When nearly cold stir in one pint of brandy and one pint of wine. If these are not liked use syrup from pickles or pears or unfermented grape juice. Pack in a large stone crock or seal in Mason jars and keep covered in a cool place. Will keep good all winter. Half of this recipe will suffice for the winter for a small family. Considering that the mince meats put up in cartons and packages contain no meat and often an inferior grade of dried apples, it certainly pays to make mince meat at home out of fresh material, when butchering is done and apples are cheapest.—Mrs. Whitehead.

MINCE MEAT. (Small jar for small family.) Two cups chopped boiled meat, or of hamburger steak, steamed tender in a double boiler, four cups of chopped apples, one pint of sweet cider or of juice from pickled peaches, one cup molasses, two cups sugar (scant), juice of three lemons, one cup shredded or chopped suet or one half cupful of butter or sweet drippings, one teaspoon of salt, mixed spices to suit taste. Cook five minutes. When ready for pie thin the mixture with cider or with a glass of tart jelly melted and add seeded raisins or currants and a little brandy if liked. Bake between two crusts of pastry and serve warm. One heaping cup of mince meat will make one pie. Fruit juice left from canned fruit is nice added to mince meat and often can be nicely utilized this way.

NEOPOLITANS.—Take pie crust left over after mixing pie. Roll it into a thin sheet and cut into oblong strips three by two inches. Bake in quick oven. Spread half with jam, lay balance of strips over that like sandwiches and spread jam or jelly on top. Dust with powdered sugar. Lemon or orange cake filling or frosting may be used instead of juice or marmolade, and crushed fresh, sweetened berries make a good filling and covering if capped with whipped cream.

ENGLISH CHEESE PIE.—One cupful of thick sour cream or milk curd, salted slightly, two beaten eggs, three fourths cup of sweet milk, one half cup sugar, one half cupful of English currants (dried). Rub curd thoroughly first and mix with other ingredients. Bake in a deep pie tin lined with pie crust. Powder with cinnamon.

FRENCH TART.—Pound eight macaroons fine, pour boiling milk over them to make a soft batter, add six well beaten eggs and one half cupful of sugar. Cook thick, add one half cup of butter and the juice of an orange. Line a pie with pastry, fill with the mixture and bake. Dust with powdered sugar before serving. Eight good sized macaroons will take from two to three cups of milk.

PATTIES.—Three cups flour, one cup lard, three fourths cup of ice water, one teaspoon baking powder, one teaspoon salt. Mix and roll like pie crust. Bake in patty pans. Makes thirty patties.

Fancy Desserts

"They make maple syrup out of corn cobs that you can't tell from the adulterated." Abe Martin.

SPONGE CAKE DESSERT.—Take hot water sponge cake, cut it into thin slices and line the sides of stem sherbet glasses. Fill in with sweetened strawberries and whipped cream.—Mrs. Southard, demonstration fancy desserts.

SPONGE CIRCLES.—Cut round pieces of sponge cake. Lay a border of sweetened strawberries around the edge of each piece of cake and fill in the center with ice cream.—Mrs. Southard, demonstration fancy desserts.

PEACH CUSTARD.—Bake a custard pie. Slice and sugar nice ripe peaches. Spread the peaches on top of the custard and cap with whipped cream.—Mrs. Southard, demonstration of fancy desserts.

PINEAPPLE DESSERT.—Thick slice of canned, or of fresh sugared pineapple, heap each slice with sweetened whipped cream flavored with a dash of vanilla and powder lightly with chopped nuts. Serve with cake.—Mrs. Southard, demonstration fancy desserts.

STRAWBERRY SPONGE.—One quart strawberries, one half package Knox gelatine, one and one half cups water, one cup sugar, juice of one lemon, whites of four eggs. Soak gelatine until soft in one cup water. Mash strawberries, add half of sugar. Boil balance of sugar with the water twenty minutes. Rub strawberries through a sieve. Add gelatine to the strawberry juice and the hot, thin syrup. Remove from fire, add berry pulp and lemon juice and beat five minutes in dish set in ice water. Add whites of eggs and beat until mixture thickens. Other berries, crushed peaches, plums and other fruits may be used the same way. Serve with cream or with custard sauce.—Mrs. Southard, domestic science demonstration of fancy desserts.

WHISKEY SPONGE PUDDING.—One quart sweet cream, yolks of ten eggs, one package gelatine, one small cup whiskey, one large cup sugar, one teaspoon vanilla. Dissolve the gelatine and beat well with the eggs, then add half of the cream, boiled, add sugar, vanilla and whiskey, and the rest of the cream whipped stiff. Allow to stand until cold and thick; at least six or eight hours.

SAUCE.—One glass of jelly, one half cup sugar, one cup water. When boiling thicken very little with corn starch. Use cold.—Mrs. Aaron J. Bessie.

COFFEE GELATINE.—One and one half cups milk, one cup cold coffee, two thirds cup sugar, three eggs beaten separately, one pinch of salt, one rounded tablespoonful of granulated gelatine, one half teaspoon of vanilla. Put the milk, coffee and gelatine in a double boiler, add sugar, salt and beaten yolks. Cook till it thickens or starts to separate, stirring occasionally. Take from fire. Add vanilla, add beaten whites of eggs, stir and turn into a mold which has been dipped in cold water.—Mrs. Creaser.

MAPLE MOUSSE.—Four eggs beaten stiff, one cup maple syrup. Cook until it thickens, then beat until cool. One pint whipped cream, beaten together.—Mrs. Schollander.

BUTTERCUP JELLY.—Dissolve one box of Knox gelatine in one pint of cold water. Add three cupfuls of boiling water, one and one half cupfuls of sugar and the juice of four lemons and two oranges. Cook five minutes and strain through cheese cloth. Divide into two portions. Add the beaten yolks of three eggs to one portion and one half cupful of chopped nuts. Add one half pint of cream to the other portion and whip until stiff or the beaten whites of two eggs if you haven't cream. Place in moulds. Cut the white jelly into cubes and heap them at the base of the yellow mold. Serve with whipped cream which may be capped with chopped pineapple. Maraschino cherries or fresh strawberries.—Mrs. Whitehead, pudding demonstration.

FRUIT GELATINE PUDDING.—Juice of three lemons, one pint of cold water, one and one half pints boiling water, one cup sugar, one box Knox gelatine. Soak gelatine in the cold water, pour on boiling water, add other ingredients. Strain and turn over mixed sliced and sugared fruits and nuts, and serve with sweetened whipped cream flavored with vanilla.—Mrs. Whitehead, pudding demonstration.

CARAMEL PUDDING.—Put pint of milk in double boiler. When hot add three heaping teaspoons of corn starch dissolved in one third cup cold milk. Add pinch of salt. Take one and one third cups of brown sugar and put in pan on stove and melt, stirring continuously to prevent scorching. When melted add very slowly one third cup boiling water. Now stir this into the thickened milk. Cook for half an hour stirring very often. Add beaten eggs five minutes before taking off stove. Serve with whipped cream.—Mrs. G. A. McIntosh.

SNOW PUDDING.—Pour one pint of boiling water on one half a box of gelatine; add the juice of one lemon and two cups of sugar. When nearly cold strain; add the whites of three eggs beaten to a froth, beat the whole together, put in mold and set on ice. With the yolks of three eggs, one pint of milk, one large teaspoon of corn starch, make a boiled custard, flavor to suit taste. Serve cold by pouring the custard around portions of the snow placed in saucers.—L. W.

CARAMEL CUSTARD.—Put one cup of sugar in a skillet and let it melt and brown, stirring constantly. When it smokes, add one cup boiling water and cook to a thick syrup. Four eggs beaten with one half cup sugar, add one quart milk and a little vanilla. Pour the syrup in the bottom of custard cups, turn in the custard and bake, set in a pan of boiling water. As soon as the custard will cut clean with a knife it is done. Too much sugar and too much cooking makes custard "watery."—Mrs. Whitehead.

ORANGE AND BANANA COMPOTE.—For six bananas a little underripe make a syrup of one cup of sugar and a half cup of water. Flavor with six whole cloves and one inch stick cinnamon. Boil eight minutes without stirring. Add the bananas and simmer until they begin to clear. Put in the juice of two oranges, a half lemon and a half glass of grape juice. Remove the cloves and cinnamon and serve on rounds of toast or sponge cake with whipped cream.

PRUNE WHIP.—(Dessert.) Take about twenty four well cooked prunes, remove pits and chop up pulp. Add one heaping tablespoon sugar, three eggs, whites and yolks beaten separately and half teaspoon vanilla. Beat all together thoroughly and pour in buttered baking dish. Bake in moderate oven thirty or thirty five minutes. This makes enough for a family of four.—Mrs. Monroe.

BANANA SHORT CAKE.—One cup sugar, one fourth cup butter, three eggs, one half cup milk, one and one third cups flour, one and one half teaspoons baking powder, flavoring. About one hour before serving slice six bananas, add one and one half cups sugar, juice of two lemons, four tablespoons water. Stir three times. When ready to serve put between layers, add chopped walnuts and heap whipped cream over all.—Mrs. D. E. Plier.

CREAM PUFFS.—One half cup melted butter, one cup hot water, cup flour, stir the flour into the water and butter while boiling. It will not lump. Let stand until cold, then stir in separately with a fork three eggs not beaten. Bake in greased gem pans or drop in greased pans and bake thirty minutes. When cold open at side and fill with stiffly beaten cream sweetened and flavored.—Contributed.

STRAWBERRY BAVARIAN CREAM.—Scald one cupful of milk or thin cream, pour it slowly over one egg yolk slightly beaten with one quarter cupful of sugar, return to double boiler, add one half tablespoonful of granulated gelatine dissolved in one quarter cupful of cold water; stir until mixture coats the spoon, strain at once into a bowl. When cool and beginning to show signs of stiffening beat in one half cupful of strawberries which have been mashed and sweetened with a tablespoonful of sugar, then fold in the stiffly beaten white of an egg and finally one half cupful of cream, whipped very stiff. Fill wet molds and leave on ice three hours. Serve with or without whipped cream.

STRAWBERRY CHARLOTTE.—Whip one cupful of cream very stiff. Beat the white of one large egg or two small ones very stiff. Beat into the white one half cupful of fine sugar. Combine this with the whipped cream, then lightly stir in one cupful of strawberries cut in quarters. Spoon into a mold lined with lady fingers or slices of sponge cake and place on ice for one hour.

ANOTHER STRAWBERRY CHARLOTTE.—Mash one cupful of strawberries and sweeten according to the acidity of the berry. Let stand to draw the juice, an hour, then strain. Dissolve one level tablespoonful of granulated gelatine in two tablespoonfuls of cold water. Set the bowl containing it in a pan of hot water and stir until smooth, add it to the strained strawberry. Now whip one cupful of cream, sweetened with two level tablespoonfuls of sugar, lightly fold the strawberry gelatine in, a few drops at a time. Turn into a wet mold and put on ice for two hours. If carefully mixed there will be no settling at the bottom. The mold for this need not be lined with cake, but a delicate wafer of some sort, preferably vanilla, should be served with it if it is molded plain.

LEMON JELLY.—Soak one box Knox sparkling gelatine in one pint cold water, two minutes; add two pints boiling water, one and one half cups sugar, and stir until dissolved; add juice of three lemons, strain through jelly bag into molds.

CHOCOLATE BLANC MANGE.—One half box Knox sparkling gelatine, one quart sweet milk, one half cup cold water, one cup sugar, two ounces grated chocolate. Soak the gelatine in the cold water; boil the sweet milk with sugar and grated chocolate and a little salt, five minutes; then add dissolved gelatine, stirring constantly; flavor with vanilla, and pour into mold; serve with whipped cream.

PINEAPPLE JELLY.—Read this recipe carefully and follow instructions. Soak one box Knox gelatine in one pint cold water, set on stove in double boiler to dissolve; when gelatine is cold and beginning to set, beat into it pineapple juice and pineapple, and place on ice to harden. Be sure you follow the above, for if you mix pineapple and its syrup with gelatine when you first make it, the acid in it will digest the gelatine so it will not harden.

WINE JELLY.—Soak one box Knox sparkling gelatine in one half pint cold water two minutes, add one quart boiling water, one and one half cups sugar, and stir until dissolved; add one half pint wine and juice of two lemons; strain and pour into mold.

NUT CREAMS.—Soak two large tablespoons of gelatine in one half cup milk. Set in hot water until melted, but do not heat. Whip one pint cream, reserving a cupful after it is whipped. Turn the gelatine into the cream adding one half teaspoonful of sugar, the beaten white of an egg, a teaspoon of vanilla and a large cup of chopped hickory and walnuts. Whip until stiff. Mold in small cups that have been wet with cold water. When ready to serve turn on a flat dish, put on remainder of whipped cream and sprinkle with chopped nuts.—Mrs. Alleman.

MAPLE CREAM GELATINE.—One half package Knox gelatine dissolved in one cup cold water; one cup maple syrup heated to boiling point, mix with gelatine, strain through a cloth and cool. Beat one pint of cream, mix in and add one cup nuts.—Mrs. Schollander.

BROD TORTE.—One cupful of rye breadcrumbs, eight eggs, a cupful of granulated sugar, one quarter pound of almonds, sliced or ground, (I prefer them sliced), one quarter pound of citron, sliced thin; one half ounce of bitter chocolate (grated), a lemon, juice and rind; one teaspoonful of ground cinnamon, one half teaspoonful of cloves, a wineglassful of brandy. Dry the bread in the oven and put through food grinder or sifter. Mix almonds, citron, chocolate and spices with the crumbs. Beat the yolks of the eggs with the sugar until thick; add lemon juice and heat again. Mix the dry ingredients with beaten eggs and sugar; next put in the brandy and, lastly, the whites of four eggs beaten stiff, are folded into the mixture. (Reserve the other four for the meringue. Pour into a "spring form" and bake in a moderate oven. When the "torte" is done, spread jelly on the top and the meringue made with the reserved eggs upon the jelly. Put back into the oven until the meringue is lightly colored.

GERMAN PAN CAKES FOR DESSERT OR LUNCH.—Beat yolks of six eggs and then beat whites of three to a stiff froth. Mix with three fourths cup grated bread crumbs, one cup cream and a large cupful of flour, pour in a buttered sauce pan, sprinkle with sugar and stir over the fire until thick then fry in butter, on a hot skillett, like pan cakes. Put on a hot dish, sift powdered sugar on them and sprinkle with lemon juice and serve hot.—Contributed.

FRUIT TRIFLE.—Beat whites of six eggs light, add six tablespoons of sugar and beat about half an hour then beat in one cupful of grated pineapple or cut up fresh strawberries or fresh raspberries or cut up fresh, ripe peaches or apricots or any fruit jam or jelly and beat five minutes. Serve ice cold in sherbet glasses as it is or chopped with flavored whipped cream. "Trifle" is sometimes made by using whipped cream, sweetened, and adding one cupful of cut up fresh berries, or peaches or orange pulp or bananas chopped, or half a glass of any fruit, jam or any jelly cut into small pieces. Beat it through the whipped cream. This is a simple and palatable dessert which can be quickly made.—Mrs. Whitehead.

JUNKET.—One quart of warm milk, two tablespoons brandy; wine or vanilla; two tablespoons sugar, one junket tablet or one tablespoon of rennet. Stir well together, then let it stand undisturbed until thick, then place on ice. Serve with sugar, nutmeg and cream. This is another dainty and easily made dessert.—Mrs. Whitehead.

Ice Cream, Sherbets, Ices and Frozen Dainties

"Which is not amiss to cool a man's stomach this hot weather."—Shakespeare.

ICE CREAM.—In packing the freezer use rock salt and crush the ice very fine. Put it in a heavy grain sack and pound and mash until nearly as fine as snow. Measure ice and salt allowing four parts ice to one of salt or ten pounds of ice to three of salt. Pack ice in layers three inches deep, then shake over one large saucerful of salt, then another three inch layer of ice and more salt, alternating ice and salt until you reach top of can. Pack the can with cream, put on the top of freezer, and let cream stand until it freezes on edges, then turn the dasher slowly for ten minutes, then quickly until cream is frozen thick but not too hard. Remove the dasher, put on the top and cork, repack freezer with ice, cover with heavy carpet and let cream ripen two or three hours.—Mrs. C. H. McKay.

ICE CREAM.—Without cooking. Two quarts of thick cream, two cups sugar. Mix and stand until sugar dissolves. Flavor to suit taste and freeze.—Mrs. C. H. McKay.

CARAMEL ICE CREAM.—Beat three eggs, one cup sugar and one half cup of flour together and cook with one pint rich milk. Brown one cupful of granulated sugar to a caramel and add to this hot custard. Cool and add one quart thick cream. Freeze.—Mrs. C. H. McKay.

CHOCOLATE ICE CREAM.—Let one large pint of milk come to a boil, add one cup of sugar and one third cup of flour mixed with the beaten yolks of three eggs; three fourths cake of sweet chocolate. Cook until thick and creamy, stirring constantly. Cool and add one quart of cream, one cup sugar and pinch of salt. Add vanilla flavoring and freeze. When partly frozen add the beaten whites of the eggs and freeze until firm but not too hard. Pack freezer well, cover and let it ripen two or three hours if possible.—Mrs. C. H. McKay.

MARYLAND ICE.—Two quarts ripe strawberries mashed with four cups sugar. Stand one hour and squeeze out the juice through a sieve or cheese cloth. Add two quarts of water and freeze. Remove water from freezer when ice is half frozen, pack, and let it stand twenty minutes. Then scoop out the center; leave wall intact. Make a filling of one pint of cream, one half cup sugar, one teaspoon flavoring beaten and whipped until stiff. Add one half cup of chopped or rolled nuts. Fill the cavity in the strawberry ice with this mixture. Repack the freezer and let it ripen four or more hours. When ready to serve, remove freezer can, wrap it in a cloth dipped in boiling water, let stand one minute when the mould of ice cream will slip out easily onto the serving platter. Serve in thick slices.—Mrs. C. H. McKay.

MOUSSE.—(Without cream.) Rub one quart of berries through a sieve, add one cupful of powdered sugar, one ounce of dissolved gelatine, and the whites of five eggs beaten stiff. Put in a mold and pack in ice and salt for three or four hours.—Mrs. C. H. McKay. (Editorial Note.—The above recipes were demonstrated by Mrs. McKay in her paper on "Ice Cream, Ices and Frozen Dainties" at Domestic Science club.)

VANILLA ICE CREAM.—One quart thick cream, seven tablespoons of sugar, one half of a vanilla bean. Cut bean into halves, scrape out seeds and mix with sugar. Add sugar to half of the cream, and put in the balance of the bean. Heat and dissolve sugar in hot cream. Remove from fire, strain and cool. Add remaining cream and freeze. The flavor of the bean makes delicious ice cream but of course good vanilla extract may be substituted. Use a tablespoon of extract. Plain ice cream is nice served with hot chocolate caramel sauce or with maple sauce and chopped nuts.—Mrs. Whitehead.

CHOCOLATE CARAMEL SAUCE.—One and one half cups brown sugar, one half cup of milk, four ounces of chocolate. Stir all together on back of range until chocolate is melted and smooth; then boil until it forms a soft ball when tried in cold water. Serve hot over the ice cream. Makes a nice pudding sauce also and is nice on cream puffs or eclairs.—Mrs. Whitehead.

RED RASPBERRY ICE CREAM.—Follow directions for chocolate ice cream given above, omitting the chocolate and adding one quart of ripe red raspberries pressed through a sieve and sweetened, when the cream is half frozen, and when the meringue is added also. Proceed with the freezing and ripen two or more hours before serving. Strawberries, apricots and peaches are equally as good used this way.—Mrs. Whitehead.

TORTONI ICE CREAM.—Boil one and one half cups sugar with water to cover until it threads from the spoon. Pour it over the stiffly beaten whites of three eggs and beat well. Scald one quart of new milk and add beaten yolks of eggs. Cool and mix with one pint of cream (may be whipped but isn't necessary) and six crumbled almond macaroons. Flavor with vanilla or almond extract. Mix all together and freeze. Cocoanut may be used in place of macaroons but it should be sprinkled with sugar and slightly browned in the oven first.—Mrs. Whitehead.

MAPLE MOUSSE.—Boil a cupful of maple syrup three minutes and stir into the beaten yolks of three eggs. Put back in dish syrup was boiled in and boil two minutes. Cool. Whip a quart of cream and add the cooled mixture and freeze. Do not stir. In the winter it may be simply set out of doors, or may be packed in ice and salt.—Mrs. G. A. McIntosh.

CARAMEL PUDDING.—Take one and one third cups of brown sugar and put in pan on stove and melt, stirring constantly to prevent burning. When melted add very slowly one third cup of boiling water.—Mrs. G. A. McIntosh.

Cold Desserts

MAPLE MOUSSE.—Four eggs beaten stiff, one cup of maple syrup. Cook until it thickens, then beat until cool. Then add one pint of whipped cream, pack in salt and ice for several hours.

FROZEN RICE PUDDING.—One cup rice, one quart milk, one quarter teaspoon salt, one cup sugar, one cup cream, one teaspoon flavoring. Cook rice in milk until soft, add sugar, salt and flavoring and pour into freezer when cold. Whip cream and add to the mixture when nearly frozen.—Mrs. Schollander.

Fruit, Ices or Sherbets

LEMON SHERBET.—One pound of sugar and one quart of water boiled to thin syrup and when cool add the grated rind of two lemons and the juice of six. For a water ice stir it now and then in the freezer and freeze slowly until like wet snow. For a sherbet freeze quickly until light and stiff. For a sorbet, add a meringue made of the beaten white of egg and sugar to the partially frozen ice.

ORANGE SHERBET.—Add the juice of six oranges and grated rind of three and the juice of one lemon to the above sugar and water syrup and freeze.

PINEAPPLE SHERBET.—Add one pint of grated pineapple and juice of one lemon to above syrup and freeze rapidly.

MINT SHERBET.—Pound the leaves of two dozen stalks of mint to a pulp, add to the syrup as above with the juice of two lemons and freeze or use mint extract.

GRAPE SHERBET.—Add the juice of one lemon and a pint of grape juice to the above syrup and freeze.

BERRY SHERBET.—Add one pint of the berry juice and juice of two lemons to above syrup and freeze.

CRANBERRY SHERBET.—One pint of strained and sweetened cooked cranberry juice and the juice of two lemons added to above syrup and freeze stiff. Fruit jellies may be melted and strained and used as substitutes for the fresh fruit juice.

FROZEN STRAWBERRIES.—Mash one quart of berries, add one and one half cups sugar and the juice of one lemon. Let it stand one hour, then add one pint of water and freeze like ice cream. Serve in punch glasses with whipped cream. Peaches and apricots are also nice frozen likewise as are cooked cranberries pressed through a colander.

FRAPPE.—This is strictly speaking of drink partially frozen until like wet snow. Grape Frappe is frozen coffee and lemon Frappe is partly frozen lemonade. A punch is merely a cold fruit drink with a block of ice floating in it. It is usually made of a combination of fruit juices sweetened and wines and liquors are frequently added to it.

PARFAIT AND MOUSSE.—This is frozen whipped cream, sweetened and flavored to suit the taste. It is packed in a mould and buried in crushed ice and salt for several hours. The cream should be frozen one and one half inches deep. The center remains soft. The opening of the mould should be bound with a strip of muslin dipped in melted suet or butter. Quick parfait is made by adding whipped cream to ice cream. At serving time beat in the whipped cream. Coffee ice cream with whipped cream is much liked, as are chocolate and caramel ice cream served this way. Macaroon mousse is made by adding crushed and rolled macaroons to whipped cream and burying the mould in ice and salt. Chopped nuts are used the same way and crushed fruit.

LEMON ICE.—Two and three fourths cups sugar, two tablespoons corn starch; add one quart boiling water. When cool add juice of eight lemons and when half frozen add whites of three eggs and one pint thick cream.—Mrs. D. E. Plier.

CURRANT ICE.—One pint currant juice (or two glasses of currant jelly), two lemons and one orange, three cups sugar, two quarts water. Pour juices over sugar and stir until dissolved then add water and freeze. The whites of two eggs may be added just before the freezing is completed.—Mrs. Schollander.

PINEAPPLE SHERBET.—One quart of granulated sugar, and one quart cold water brought to a boil. Pour over one quart can of grated pineapple and juice of six lemons. Strain and put into freezer. When cold add whites of three eggs beaten stiff with one tablespoon of sugar. Freeze.—Mrs. W. S. Davidson.

PISTACHO MOUSSE.—Whip a pint of cream very stiff, beat into it lightly four tablespoonfuls of powdered sugar; flavor to taste with pistacho extract and stir in one half cupful of chopped nuts. Last of all color a delicate green with vegetable coloring mixture. Turn all cream into a mould and pack with ice and salt for four hours.—Mrs. J. D. Wolpert.

STRAWBERRY ICE CREAM.—Three cupfuls of cream and one of milk, or one quart of thin cream, three quarters of a cupful of sugar; scald, but do not boil. Beat until cold, add one cupful of strawberries mashed with their juice and one half cupful of sugar. Place in freezer, pack in ice and salt, using three quarters ice and one quarter salt, and freeze until as stiff as can be turned. Remove dasher, work up and down with a long handled spoon to pack solidly and set aside for twenty minutes or longer. Serve garnished with a half cupful of strawberries cut in two. For individual servings a simple way is to pack the ice cream in pound or half pound baking powder tins after it has been frozen and bury it in ice and salt. It then may be turned out and sliced in rounds, one round to a person, and the strawberries used to decorate each service. Of course, if this is done the cream must be very firm and should be packed at least two hours before it is used. To avoid much melting the bucket may be put in the ice box in a tin pan.

STRAWBERRY MOUSSE.—Dissolve one tablespoonful of granulated gelatine in one quarter cupful of water by placing the bowl containing it in a pan of hot water; when smooth add three quarters of a cupful of powdered sugar and stir until cool. Strain gradually into two cupfuls of cream whipped very stiff, add one cupful of fresh strawberries which have been chopped fine with a silver knife and sugared with one third cupful of sugar. Have the mould already packed in ice and salt, put the mousse into it by the spoonful, first being sure that all the ingredients are well mixed; cover with buttered paper, put on the lid of one mould and pile ice and salt on top. Put in a cold place for two to four hours. Unmold and serve with halved strawberries and sponge cake or angels food.

ORANGE WATER ICE.—Juice of six oranges, two teaspoons extract of orange, juice of one lemon, one quart water, one pound powdered sugar, one gill rich, sweet cream, add all together and strain. Freeze same as ice cream.—Mrs. H. J. Liddell.

LEMON SHERBET WITH CREAM.—Mix four large cups of sugar with three level tablespoons of flour and stir in two quarts of boiling water and cook thick. Cool and add the juice of one dozen lemons. Strain and freeze. When half frozen add one pint of cream whipped stiff with half a cupful of sugar and add the beaten whites of two eggs. Stir well through the half frozen sherbet and finish freezing. When firm, remove the dasher from the freezer, repack and cover freezer with a carpet or heavy blanket. Let it ripen two hours or more. Makes one gallon of sherbet.—Mrs. Whitehead.

LEMON SHERBET.—Juice of three or four lemons, according to size, two cups sugar, one quart of fresh sweet milk. Mix lemon juice and sugar and put them in the freezer and let stand while you pack freezer, quickly stir in ice cold milk and freeze quickly. The milk must be fresh morning's milk and it must commence to freeze immediately or it will curdle. Grated pineapple may be added to this if liked. After it is frozen the beaten whites of two eggs mixed with two tablespoons of sugar, should be stirred through the sherbet and left to ripen until serving time. Cream may be used instead of milk but half of it should be scalded with half of the sugar and cooled before mixing with the lemon juice.—Mrs. Whitehead.

HOT CHOCOLATE SAUCE FOR ICE CREAM.—Two cups of light brown sugar, 2 tablespoons of chocolate, ½ cup sweet milk, butter size of a walnut. Boil until it forms a soft ball when dropped in cold water. Do not beat. Flavor with vanilla and let it stand a moment, pour the sauce on ice cream in the dishes just before serving. Maple sauce is made the same way substituting maple sugar for the brown and omitting the chocolate. Caramel sauce is made by browning sugar in a hot skillet until it melts and smokes and then adding the sweet milk and butter and cooking to soft ball stage. Minced nuts may be sprinkled over the sauce on top of ice cream.—Mrs. Whitehead.

STRAWBERRY FRAPPE.—For one quart of ripe berries use four lemons, three cupfuls of sugar and three pints of water. Crush the berries with the sugar, and let them stand an hour before adding the juice of the lemons and the water. Mix well, pour into a freezer and stir for fifteen or twenty minutes. Pack in ice for an hour or two and serve in glasses with or without whipped cream on top.

MELON SHERBET.—Boil one pint of water with half a pound of sugar for twenty minutes, then stir in a little gelatine melted in cold water. Add the strained juice of two lemons, half a pint of melon juice and then the beaten whites of two eggs. Whisk all together and partially freeze.

ANGEL FRAPPE.—Dip half a pound of lump sugar in the strained juice of some white currants and boil them to the "thread" point. Beat the whites of two eggs till stiff, then pour on the sugar and continue beating. Whip a pint of double cream, add a quarter of a pint of currant juice, mix all quickly together and freeze without stirring until nearly solid. Serve in tall glasses with a few white currants in the bottom of each.

Puddings and Pudding Sauces

"Since Eve ate apples much depends upon dinner."—Lord Byron.

ENGLISH PLUM PUDDING.—Two cups sugar, five eggs, one nutmeg, one tablespoon salt, one quart sweet milk, one loaf bread without crusts, one large piece citron chopped, four cups suet, two cups currants, four heaping cups raisins, three pints flour. This makes a large pudding and if cooked in one mould, must boil ten hours.—Mrs. Mary Harvey.

BROWN BETTY PUDDING.—Take stale pieces of bread and lightly brown them in oven until thoroughly dry and crisp. With rolling pin crush the bread into small crumbs. Put into pudding dish a layer of these crumbs, then a layer of apples, and arrange in layers until dish is full, last layer crumbs. Flavor with sugar, cinnamon, lemon and butter on each layer and bake slowly. Serve with sweet sauce, cream or milk.—Mrs. Mary Harvey.

SUET PUDDING.—One cup chopped suet, one cup raisins, one cup brown sugar, two tablespoons syrup, one tablespoon soda, salt, and one egg, three cups flour, one teaspoon cinnamon. Steam from two to three hours and serve with pudding dip made of one cup sugar, scant, one tablespoon butter, two tablespoons flour, one cup boiling water, flavor to taste.—Mrs. D. E. Plier.

PLUM PUDDING.—One and one half pounds suet, one pound stoned raisins, one pound currants, eight eggs, one and one half nutmeg, two ounces candied peel, one teaspoon ground ginger, one half pound bread crumbs, one half pound flour, two pounds of dark sugar, one half pint milk.—Mrs. A. McKay.

SPONGE PUDDING.—Two large tablespoons sugar, two large tablespoons butter, four large tablespoons flour, six eggs, two cups sweet milk. Let milk scald, while hot add butter, then sugar, then flour mixed with cold milk. Stir well until it boils, remove from the fire, add yolks well beaten, then add whites beaten stiff. Pour into buttered dish, set in pan of hot water and bake one hour. Half of this will serve six people.—Mrs. Schollander.

ANGEL PUDDING.—Two eggs, one cup of sugar, one cup of chopped walnuts, one cup of dates, two tablespoons flour, one teaspoon baking powder. Bake twenty minutes, serve with hard sauce or whipped cream.—Mrs. Schollander.

SNOW BALLS.—One half cup of butter, one half cup milk, one cup sugar, one and one quarter cups flour, three and one half teaspoons baking powder, whites of four eggs. Cream butter, add sugar gradually, then milk. Add flour mixed and sifted with baking powder, then add the whites of eggs beaten stiff. Steam thirty five minutes. Serve with orange sauce. Orange sauce. Whites of three eggs, one cup of powdered sugar, juice and rind of two oranges and juice of one lemon. Beat whites until stiff, add sugar gradually, and continue beating. Add rind and fruit juices.—Mrs. Schollander.

PRUNE PUDDING.—Whites of six eggs, beaten stiff, and one cup of sugar. Boil and pit twenty prunes and chop fine. Mix all and bake forty minutes. Serve with whipped cream.—Mrs. R. J. Walker.

CHOCOLATE PUDDING.—One half cup sugar, a piece of butter the size of an egg, one heaping teaspoon baking powder, one egg, one half cup milk, one cup flour, two squares of chocolate grated. Bake as a cake and serve cold. Sauce: Yolks of two eggs and one cup of sugar beaten to a cream, one half cup of cream, whipped, whites of two eggs, beaten stiff, and added last. Flavor with vanilla.—Mrs. C. C. Mackenroth.

ANGEL PUDDING.—Two eggs, one cup sugar, one cup chopped nuts, one cup dates, two tablespoons flour, one teaspoon baking powder, bake twenty minutes, serve with whipped cream.—Mrs. Schollander.

CORN PUDDING.—Score the rows of corn in a dozen big ears and press out the juice and pulp. To two cups of pulp, add two well beaten eggs, one tablespoon of butter, one small teaspoon of salt, a dash of pepper and two scant cups of sweet milk. Bake in a greased pudding dish until firm and brown. Serve with hard sauce made by creaming half a cup of butter with one cupful of sugar until light, add a dash of nutmeg and put a tablespoon of sauce on each piece of hot pudding.—Mrs. Whitehead, Southern Cookery Demonstration.

PRUNE WHIP.—One pound prunes, cook until tender, put through colander (to remove pits) add half cup sugar, when cold add the whites of four eggs, well beaten; beat all together, put dish in oven four minutes. Serve cold, with whipped cream. This amount will serve six to eight people.—Mrs. Liddell.

ENGLISH PLUM PUDDING.—One pound chopped suet, one pound chopped raisins, one pound English currants, one ounce citron and lemon peel, six eggs, three cups of bread crumbs, three cups dark brown sugar, one teaspoon of cloves, cinnamon and nutmeg, one pint of sweet milk. Mix all well together, then add flour until the consistency of fruit cake. Tie it in a strong, new cloth, allowing room to swell, and boil it in a kettle of boiling water constantly for six hours.—Mrs. Eleanor Wilkinson.

LEMON PUDDING.—Slice one large or two small lemons in a pudding dish with one and one half cups hot water, one cup sugar, and one tablespoon butter. Set on stove to get warm while you prepare batter, by mixing one half teaspoon butter, one half cup sugar, yolks of two eggs, one quarter cup sweet milk, one teaspoon baking powder, three fourths cup sifted flour. Pour over the lemons and bake. When done cover with a meringue and brown.—Mrs. A. D. Paulson.

MOTHER'S BOILED INDIAN PUDDING.—Two cupfuls of corn meal, one cupful of flour, three teaspoons of baking powder or two level spoons of soda, one half cup of molasses, two beaten eggs, one tablespoon of salt, and enough sweet or sour milk (if soda is used) to make a thin batter. Turn into a floured, wet pudding bag or into a greased double boiler and boil steadily from two to three hours. Serve with cream and sugar alone, or spiced with nutmeg, or with any favorite pudding sauce.—Mrs. Whitehead.

CHOCOLATE PUDDING WITH RAISINS.—Sauce: One cup sifted flour, one and one half level teaspoons baking powder, one half teaspoon cinnamon, one quarter teaspoon salt. Sift several times. Beat one yolk of egg with one third cup sugar, three tablespoons melted butter and one quarter cup milk. Stir into the flour mixture then beat in two squares of chocolate melted over hot water; add beaten white of egg, and steam half an hour in buttered cups. Raisin sauce: Chop one half cup raisins and stew in a little water then add one half cup sugar and cook to a thick syrup, then thin with hot water, one half cup, and serve.—Mrs. Whitehead, pudding demonstration.

RAISIN SAUCE.—Stew one cup seeded raisins in one pint of water until soft. Mash them and strain them through cheese cloth. Put the liquor on to boil, add one tablespoon lemon and sugar to taste. Thicken with one tablespoon corn starch wet in cold water, and cook until smooth. Add one tablespoon of butter just before serving.

PEACH COBBLER.—Two cups flour, two teaspoons baking powder, one half teaspoon salt, one half beaten egg mixed with three fourths cup milk, one quart sweetened peaches. Mix dry ingredients like pie crust, add milk and egg, roll out, line greased pudding pan, fill in with sweetened fruit. Cover with crust and bake.—Mrs. Whitehead, pudding demonstration.

FRENCH APPLE PUDDING.—Two cups of flour, two teaspoons baking powder, one half teaspoon salt, one cup sugar, two cups milk, one half cup butter, two eggs. Cream butter and sugar, add eggs, beat, add milk and other ingredients. Butter deep pan, fill it with peeled and quartered cooking apples. Cover with sugar and cinnamon or grated nutmeg. Turn the batter over it and bake brown. Invert the pudding pan and serve with cream and sugar, or pudding sauce.

STEAMED APPLE PUDDING.—(In cups.) Fill cups half full of prepared apples, sugared, buttered and spiced to taste. Make a drop batter of one cup flour sifted with one teaspoon baking powder, one quarter teaspoon of salt and mixed soft with sweet milk. Fill cups with batter and steam three quarters of an hour. Serve with lemon or vinegar sauce, made as follows: One tablespoon each of butter, flour and sugar, stirred over the fire together, add boiling water, about one pint, and cook thick. Season with one tablespoon vinegar, lemon juice or vanilla.—Mrs. Whitehead, pudding demonstration.

STRAWBERRY PUDDING SAUCE.—Cream one half cupful of butter and two cupfuls of sugar until very light, gradually add one pint of crushed strawberries and serve with bread, tapioca or rice pudding.

LEMON HONEY SAUCE.—Cream one half cup of butter with one cupful of sugar and add yolks of three eggs. Beat together and cook in double boiler, add slightly beaten whites of eggs and juice of two lemons. When cold add one half pint of whipped cream. Serve on gelatine or snow pudding.—Mrs. Whitehead.

FOAM SAUCE.—Three eggs beaten light with one cupful of sugar, add one teaspoonful of butter, one teaspoonful of vanilla and one tablespoonful of brandy or whiskey or orange juice if liquor is not liked. Just before serving add one cupful of boiling water. Serve with suet or plum pudding.

ANOTHER FOAM SAUCE.—One beaten egg, one half cup sugar, three tablespoons boiling milk, flavor with vanilla.

ENGLISH SWEET SAUCE.—Yolks of two eggs, beaten with three quarters cup powdered sugar. Add one cup sweet cream and the grated rind of one orange. Cook over slow fire five minutes, stirring all of the time.

MAPLE SYRUP SAUCE FOR PUDDINGS.—Melt one tablespoon of butter and blend with half as much flour, add one half cup of hot maple syrup and cook thick. Serve as sauce on apple pudding. Brown sugar syrup may be used instead of maple syrup and caramel sugar syrup is equally as good used the same way.—Mrs. Whitehead, sauces demonstrated in paper on puddings and pudding sauces.

VANILLA SAUCE.—Norwegian. Put three pints of fresh milk in a kettle over the fire and let come to a boil (but do not let it boil). Four ounces of sugar, yolks of five eggs, beaten together about ten or fifteen minutes. Add this to the hot milk, flavor with vanilla. Get cool. To be served with fruit gelatine or sliced oranges.—Mrs. R. Meidell.

STEAMED FRUIT PUDDING.—One cupful each of molasses, bread crumbs, water, flour and currants and raisins or dates. Soak bread crumbs in the water until soft, add one beaten egg, three level tablespoons of melted butter or beef drippings, one teaspoon of soda, a little salt and cinnamon. Mix all ingredients together and steam in a greased steam cooker or double boiler for two hours. Serve with any favorite pudding sauce. As it is something like plum pudding foam sauce is liked best with it.—Mrs. Whitehead, demonstration of puddings.

CORN STARCH PUDDING.—One quart milk, eight tablespoons corn starch, pinch of salt and one half cup sugar. Heat milk to boiling point and stir in sugar, salt and corn starch mixed together. When cooked sufficiently turn over the beaten whites of two eggs and stir. To make it yellow use the yolks of eggs. Serve (without) with or without cream.—Dorothy Whitehead.

CHOCOLATE PUDDING.—One quarter cup butter, one cup sugar, yolks of two eggs, one half cup milk, one and three eighths cups of flour, three teaspoons baking powder, whites of three eggs, one and one third squares Bakers chocolate, one eighth teaspoon salt and one fourth teaspoon vanilla. Cream the butter, add one half of the sugar, beat yolks and add remaining sugar, combine mixture, add milk, flour, baking powder and salt, then add the whites beaten stiff, melted chocolate and vanilla. Bake in cake pan. Fill the center with whipped cream sweetened and flavored and pour around chocolate sauce.

CHOCOLATE SAUCE.—Boil one cup sugar, one half cup water until a thin syrup. Melt one and one half squares Bakers chocolate and pour gradually over the hot syrup.—Dorothy Whitehead, demonstrated in 7th grade Domestic Science class at school.

SUET PUDDING.—One cup chopped suet, one cup milk (or water) one cup chopped raisins, one cup molasses, two and one half cups flour, one teaspoon soda, one half teaspoon each salt, cloves, cinnamon and nutmeg. Sift flour, soda, salt and spices. Add suet and raisins. Mix milk (or water) and molasses, beat into the dry mixture and steam three hours. Dressing for pudding: One cup sugar, one egg, one tablespoon flour, two tablespoons cold water, beat well and stir in half pint boiling milk or water. Add butter size of an egg, flavor with vanilla.—Mrs. W. C. McGuiness.

NUT PUDDING.—One cup sugar, one cup butter, one cup milk, two eggs, two and one half teaspoons salt, two teaspoons baking powder, two cups flour, one cup nuts. Steam good three hours and do not uncover at all while steaming or it will fall. Eat with golden sauce. One heaping teaspoon butter, one cup powdered sugar, two egg yolks, four or six tablespoons cream, flavoring. Beat whites of two eggs well, and add last, do not boil.—Mrs. Paul Leonhardy.

STRAWBERRY SHORT CAKE.—Sift one quart of flour with three teaspoons of baking powder and a tablespoon of sugar and one half teaspoon of salt. Work in three rounding tablespoons of butter to a mealy mixture or until the butter and flour are thoroughly blended; now lightly mix in enough milk to make a soft dough, (a little over a pint). Handle just enough to roll out after the milk is added to the flour. Roll in two round or square sheets, put in greased tins, dot with butter and bake a nice brown in a quick oven. Crush two quarts of strawberries with sugar to sweeten. Build the short cake in layers with the berries between cakes and generously spread on top. The whole berries are often reserved for the top. Serve with thick cream or with sweetened whipped cream. Raspberries, grated pineapple and fresh sliced peaches or oranges are used in season as well as strawberries.—Mrs. Whitehead, demonstration Southern Cookery.

Cheese

"It seems as tho' science has condemned everything we relished when a boy. * * * We have had this pure food idea pounded into us until we can't find anything any more that 'taint tainted."—Sam Clark.

COTTAGE CHEESE.—Heat two quarts of lobbered milk slowly until curd is formed; drain through cheese cloth and when dry add one teaspoonful of salt and one half cup of sweet or sour cream.—Mrs. J. Bruegger.

CHEESE AND BREAD.—One cup bread crumbs, two cups milk, soak. Add one half pound grated cheese, one tablespoon butter, two or three eggs, beaten lightly, pepper and salt to suit taste. Brown lightly. For a small family use one half the amount.—Mrs. Davidson.

CHEESE SCALLOP.—One cup grated cheese, 2 egg yolks beaten, 2 tablespoons of melted butter, one cup bread crumbs soaked in one and one half cups milk, dash of cayenne pepper. Mix all together, then add stiffly beaten whites of eggs. Bake in a greased dish in a hot oven covering the top with fine bread crumbs.—Contributed.

CHEESE AND BREAD OMELET.—Soak a cupful of bread crumbs until soft, then drain, add a cupful of milk and three egg yolks to the bread and salt and pepper. Stir the stiffly beaten whites of eggs into the bread and one cupful of grated cheese. Cook like an omelet with butter in a hot skillet. Fold over and serve.—Contributed.

CHEESE AND MACARONI.—Boil a cupful of broken macaroni tender in boiling salted water. Make a cream sauce of two tablespoons of butter blended with as much flour and cooked with one half pint of milk. Add salt and cook thick. Then add four large tablespoons of grated cheese and one beaten egg. Mix with the drained macaroni in a baking dish, cover with crumbs and brown in the oven.—Contributed.

CHEESE SOUFFLE.—Stir one tablespoon of flour into one tablespoon of melted butter in a pan on the stove until well blended, add one cup of milk and cook until smooth. Add one cup of grated cheese and well beaten yolks of three eggs, lastly add well beaten whites of eggs and a pinch of salt. Put into a greased baking dish, set in a pan of hot water and bake about twenty minutes or until light and brown. Eat as soon as it is baked.—Contributed.

CHEESE AND POTATO OMELET.—Spread mashed potatoes an inch thick in a hot, heavy skillet with one tablespoon of hot butter or drippings. Brown on bottom and grate cheese thickly over top; add pepper. Cook and when potatoes are well browned on the bottom fold over like an omelet and serve.

ITALIAN MACARONI.—Cook a cupful of macaroni in salted water until tender. Drain off the water and put the macaroni into a colander. Have ready in a saucepan a large tablespoonful of butter, heated. Put into this a sliced onion and cook tender. Turn into the saucepan, then a can of tomatoes and one chili pepper (or in quantity according to its "hotness"). Salt and cook fifteen minutes. Arrange the macaroni alternately in layers with the tomato in a bake dish, finishing of course, with the tomatoes. Cover with grated cheese and bake fifteen or twenty minutes.

TOMATOES STUFFED WITH MACARONI AND CHEESE.—Cook one cup broken macaroni or spaghetti tender in salted water; drain and blanch in cold water. Skin light tomatoes and scoop out centers. Fill with the macaroni, dot with butter and season with salt and pepper, then cover top with grated cheese. Bake in a moderate oven thirty minutes. Serve plain or with cream sauce. For Italian macaroni, chop the tomatoes, dredge with flour and mix with the above ingredients, putting a thick layer of cheese on top. Bake until brown.—Contributed.

Beverages

"Serenely pure yet divinely strong."—Pope.

COFFEE.—Three parts Java to one part Mocha coffee ground fine together. Allow one tablespoonful of coffee to each cup of cold water. Mix in one third of a whole egg for five cups of coffee. Bring to a good boil. Remove from fire, add a dash of cold water and serve.—Mrs. C. H. McKay, demonstration of beverages.

CHOCOLATE.—One half cup grated chocolate, one half cup sugar mixed. Add to one quart of milk. Bring to a boil. Let it stand on back of range half an hour, then reheat it. Serve whipped cream in each cup.—Mrs. C. H. McKay, demonstration.

TEA.—Water for making black tea should be boiling. Allow level tablespoon tea to a pint of water. Let it stand covered three to seven minutes. Water for green tea should not be boiling hot, as green tea should be a smooth and oily beverage. The Japanese serve tea warm but not hot. Allow same proportions as above. Let it stand three minutes. Add hot water to tea leaves left in tea pot and leave again. Use an earthen tea pot always. Soft water makes better tea than hard water.—Mrs. C. H. McKay, demonstration of beverages.

CLARET FREEZE.—Claret wine to taste. Fill glass half full of chopped ice, add wine and sweeten to taste with cherry syrup. Add sliced lemon or pineapple, rose leaves, or Maraschino cherries. Serve with straws.

mixture may be frozen to a soft mush in a freezer and serve as a dinner course.—Contributed.

CHAMPAIGNE PUNCH.—Make a syrup of two cups sugar and one quart of water and make a lemonade with juice of five lemons. Add one gill brandy, one half gill Jamaica rum and one pint of champaigne. Whip white of one egg to a snow and sweeten and beat again. Mix with the punch and freeze like lemon ice, or omit the egg. Mix well and serve from punch bowl with large block of ice floating in the liquid.—Contributed.

TEMPERANCE PUNCH.—One quart strained lemonade, one pint unfermented grape juice; juice of six oranges with two cups sugar diluted in it. Mix all well together with one gallon of ice water. Taste and add more sugar if needed. Sliced or diced pineapple, cherries or any fresh fruits may be added to this in season. Have block of ice in punch bowl and stir well.

WEDDING PUNCH.—(No liquors.) One tumbler each of currant, raspberry and blackberry jelly, juice of twelve lemons, juice and pulp of two oranges, one pint grape juice, one pint of grated pineapple, one pint of preserved strawberries, one quart of canned peaches, one fourth pound conserved cherries, two pounds sugar, one quart ginger ale, three quarts water. Make syrup of the water and sugar; strain. Add all the jellies to hot syrup. When cool add strained lemon juice then the grated pineapple, orange pulp, and other fruits. Cover and stand over night. At serving time turn into punch bowl with one quart of shaved ice or a big block of clear ice. Add other ingredients, stir well and serve in punch cups or glasses.—Contributed.

WINE PUNCH.—Make a gallon of rich lemonade, strain it and add a bottle of port wine, sherry of claret. Mixed conserved cherries, pineapple and orange pulp may be stirred through this. Add a quart of shaved ice or use a big block of clear ice and stir frequently, adding water and sugar as needed or more lemonade to the drips in the bowl.

GRAPE LEMONADE.—Two quarts of sweet lemonade, one pint bottle of unfermented grape juice. Mix thoroughly and serve with ice.

FRUIT DRINK.—Use one tablespoon of diluted currant, strawberry, raspberry or grape jelly to each glass of iced water and serve with shaved ice. Or the canned fruit juice may be used instead of jelly.

GINGER ALE PUNCH.—Add to a half pint of shaved ice one tablespoon brandy, one tablespoon powdered sugar and one well beaten egg. Add half a pint of imported ginger ale. Let it stand five minutes.

BLACKBERRY CORDIAL.—One gallon of blackberry juice, add two pounds of loaf sugar, half an ounce of cloves, one ounce nutmeg, cinnamon and allspice; boil together twenty five minutes. When cold add one quart of brandy.

ORANGE PUNCH.—Dissolve one fourth pound loaf sugar in one pint boiling water; add juice of one lemon, one pint of orange juice, one half cup brandy, one half cup rum. Used either hot or cold.—Contributed.

HOT BRANDY PUNCH.—One fourth pint Jamaica rum, one half pint brandy, one quarter pound sugar, one lemon and one pint boiling water. Put sugar and lemon juice in a punch bowl or large pitcher; pour in the boiling water; add the rum and brandy and mix thoroughly. Grate nutmeg on top and serve. For mint julep add one dozen sprigs of fresh mint to the lemon juice and sugar before adding the water.—Contributed.

SHERRY FLIP.—Break an egg into a quart Mason jar, add half a can of shaved ice and one tablespoon of sugar. Fasten top securely on the can and shake hard until egg is light and foamy. Add two tablespoons of sherry wine and shake again. Serve with a grating of nutmeg.—Contributed.

FRUIT NECTAR.—Put the thinly sliced rind of three lemons in a jar with one pound of chopped raisins, and one and one half pounds of sugar. Pour two gallons of boiling water over it. When cold add juice of lemons and let stand in a cold place for a week, stirring it every day. Strain through a jelly bag until clear, then seal in bottles.

RASPBERRY SHRUB.—Place raspberries in a jar and cover with good cider vinegar, let it stand over night; next morning strain and to each pint of juice add a pint of sugar; boil ten minutes; bottle while hot. Use one half glass of the shrub to one half glass shaved ice and water. Good summer drink. Same directions for currant shrub.

MILK SHAKE.—Fill your glass two thirds full of milk, sweeten to taste with any fruit syrup, or with sugar, then flavor with vanilla or orange. Fill glass with shaved ice and shake in a covered Mason jar or a milk shaker until well mixed.

MULLED ALE.—Heat one quart of good ale with a little nutmeg; beat five eggs light and mix with a little cold ale; then pour the hot and cold ale back and forth several times to prevent curdling. Warm and stir until sufficiently thick; add a glass of brandy; strain and serve in tiny glasses.

ICED COFFEE.—Make two pints of good, strong coffee, and clear it with the beaten white and shell of an egg. Strain, sweeten, and let it get cold. Add the juice of one lemon and set the mixture in ice for an hour. Serve in cups or claret glasses with a little whipped cream on top.

TEA NECTAR.—Draw one and a half pints of strong tea for three minutes and pour off into a bowl. Sweeten to taste with sugar, the juice of a lemon and a wineglassful of brandy. Ice for an hour, decorate with thin slices of lemon cut in quarters and serve in small glasses.

ORANGE PUNCH.—Stir a cupful of sugar into a scant cup of water and simmer for half an hour. Skim and let it get cold before adding the strained juice of four oranges and half as much lemon juice. Beat all well together; fill chilled tumblers with pounded ice and pour in enough of the syrup to fill up the interstices.

Refreshing Beverages for Convalescents

FOR FEVER CONVALESCENT.—One half fresh peach, one teaspoon brandy, one tablespoon sugar, juice of half a lemon. Press through sieve and add plenty of shaved ice. Sip a little at a time.

ICED MINT.—One fourth teaspoon peppermint essence, one tablespoon of powdered sugar, one tablespoon of water, one tablespoonful of wine, one teaspoon of brandy. Mix well together, fill glass with shaved ice and sip through a straw.

STERILIZED LEMONADE.—Boil one pint of water and mix it with juice of a lemon, four lumps of sugar and grated rind of lemon. Cover and stand two hours. Strain and serve ice cold. For orangeade add juice of two oranges to above and two extra lumps of sugar.

EGG-NOG.—Scald one pint of milk, but do not boil. Beat three eggs to a froth with one fourth cup sugar, add half a gill of beet brandy and one tablespoon of rum and a little nutmeg. Beat well and add the scalded milk, either hot or cold.

LEMON WHEY.—Good to induce perspiration, to break up a cold. Boil half pint of milk and add one tablespoon of lemon juice; add more if this does not turn the milk. Let it boil up then turn into bowl to settle; strain, sweeten and add hot water to suit taste.

FRUIT JELLY DRINKS.—Melt currant, raspberry or cranberry jelly in hot water, sweeten to suit taste and set aside to cool. The juice of fresh berries is pleasing to a patient when the berries are forbidden. Strain the fruit through a fine sieve or through cheese cloth and cool with shaved ice and sweeten.

FLAX SEED TEA.—One ounce of flax seed and a little powdered licorice root and pour on a pint of hot water. Steep four hours then strain. Good for a cold.

BARLEY COFFEE.—Roast Barley until well browned and boil 1 tablespoon of it in a pint of water five minutes, strain and add a little sugar, if liked. Nourishing drink for fever convalescent.

APPLE WATER.—Roast two tart apples until soft. Pour a pint of cold water on them and stand in cold place one hour. Good for patients in fever and eruptive diseases. Do not sweeten.

Eggs

"Twelve studies in white and gold,
Oh, egg, within thy oval shell,
What palate tickling joys do dwell."

STUFFED EGGS.—Cook eggs twenty minutes just below boiling point. Remove shells, cut in half lengthwise. Take out yolks and mash them. Add one half quantity finely minced ham or chicken, moisten with one tablespoon of butter softened and seasoned with salt, pepper and mustard. Fill whites with this mixture and press halves together. Roll in fine bread crumbs, then into beaten egg and again in crumbs. Fry brown in very hot fat. Serve garnished with parsley.—Mrs. H. C. Windel.

EGGS LYONNAISE.—Boil eight eggs twenty minutes and throw in cold water and remove shells. Separate yolks and whites and chop whites fine. Put whole yolks in a dish over boiling water to keep warm. Peel and chop two medium sized onions and fry golden brown in two tablespoons of butter. Season with salt, pepper and nutmeg and add a cupful of white sauce. Stir gently to boiling point, then add chopped whites and cook two minutes. Pour over hot whole yolks, sprinkle with minced parsley and serve.—Mrs. H. C. Windel.

HAM AND EGG ON TOAST.—A good way to use small pieces of left over ham or other cooked meat is to chop them fine. Toast several slices of bread and lay on a platter. Beat three eggs slightly, pour in a little milk, cook over the fire a few minutes, but not till it is thick, stir in the chopped meat and pour over the toast.—Mrs. Geo. Farries.

ONION EGGS.—Boil six eggs hard, slice three of the eggs, cut three onions in slices, fry in butter, lay them on a platter; place the sliced eggs over them, cover to keep hot, grate the other three eggs, season with salt and pepper, boil up in a little cream and pour over the eggs and onions.—Mrs. Geo. Farries.

SHIRRED EGG.—Grease a shallow pan and break eggs carefully into it. Sprinkle with salt and pepper and heat with butter. Steam or bake until the whites are set and serve. Shirred eggs are usually served in the individual dishes they are baked in. A little minced parsley is often sprinkled over the top of each plate.

LAYER EGGS.—Fry two onions, sliced thin until they are tender and brown. Cut hard boiled eggs into slices. Add half a bowl of good gravy to the hot onions and then the eggs. Season with salt and pepper and serve.

SCRAMBLED EGG.—(New.) Break eight fresh eggs into a saucepan, add a piece of butter the size of an egg, eight tablespoons of cream; two tablespoons of soup stock, one scant teaspoon of salt and a little pepper. Set over the fire and stir until the eggs begin to thicken then remove from the fire and beat with a Dover beater until they are light and delicate. Heat over the fire again and serve in a warm dish. Very nice for breakfast and lunch.

CREAM TOAST WITH EGG.—Heat a quart of milk; toast slices of bread, butter them and dip each into the milk a second. Lay in a deep serving dish. Now add a tablespoon of butter and a pinch of salt to the hot milk. Beat the yolk of an egg, adding gradually a small tablespoon of flour and two tablespoons of cold milk. Stir into the boiling milk and cook until creamy, then pour it over and around the toast and serve immediately. May be served with poached eggs, too.

SCRAMBLED EGGS WITH ASPARAGUS TIPS.—Beat six eggs a trifle with two tablespoons of cream and scramble in hot pan. Season and stir in the tips of a bunch of stewed asparagus. Add a dash of pepper and serve on toast.

EGGS, NEW YORK STYLE.—Boil six eggs half an hour. Drop them into cold water; shell and quarter them and lay them in a buttered baking dish. Make a white sauce of one pint of hot milk with butter, and flour enough to thicken. Season and stir until smooth. Chop two large boiled onions, add to the sauce and pour over the eggs, sprinkle the top with cracker crumbs, dots of butter and two tablespoons of grated cheese. Bake until a nice brown and serve immediately.

CREOLE EGGS.—Poach eggs in deep, boiling salted water and serve with a highly seasoned tomato sauce.

CREAMED EGGS.—Poach eggs and serve with a thickened, seasoned cream sauce or a browned gravy sauce, mushrooms, asparagus tips, minced parsley or minced cold boiled ham, cauliflower, green corn, oysters, sausage or dried beef may be added to any cream sauce and served over poached eggs or hard boiled eggs, cut into slices or quartered. Or any of these sauces may be spread on an omelet, folded over and served.

CHEESE AND EGGS ON TOAST.—Beat three eggs with three tablespoons of bread crumbs, soaked soft in milk and drained. Add three tablespoons of melted butter, one teaspoon of mustard, salt and pepper and lastly one half pound of grated cheese. Spread evenly on slices of toast and brown quickly in the oven.

EGGS AND POTATOES.—Fry diced cold boiled or baked potatoes brown in a butter, seasoning with salt and pepper; break in three or four eggs and scramble lightly. Add two tablespoons of thick cream and serve immediately.

SWISS EGGS.—Line a pie plate with thin slices of cheese. Mix a cup of milk with one teaspoon of mustard, a dash of cayenne and a little salt. Pour half of this mixture over the cheese. Then break carefully five eggs on the cheese; pour over the rest of the milk and bake until the eggs are set. The cheese will melt and thicken the milk.

HONEYCOMB EGGS.—Set a granite pan with a tablespoon of butter in the oven to heat. Beat five eggs with one third cup of milk and salt and pepper exactly one minute. Pour into the hot pan and bake in a quick oven until eggs rise to the top. Serve immediately.

OMELET, NEWPORT STYLE.—Soak a pint of bread crumbs in one pint of milk. Beat eight eggs very light and stir with the crumbs, beating five minutes. Heat two tablespoons of butter in a pan, pour in the mixture, season with salt and pepper and stir and scramble the mixture quickly with the point of a knife, tossing it lightly. Cook about three minutes and serve on toast.

PLAIN OMELET.—Separate four eggs. Beat the yolks with half a cup of milk or water, season with salt and pepper. Beat the whites in a bowl very light or until the bowl can be inverted and retain the whites of eggs. Cut the whites into the yolks and turn into a hot frying pan with melted butter. Let it stand over the fire undisturbed until it is nicely browned on the bottom. Then run the pan into a hot oven and brown on top. Serve immediately with or without sauce. Vegetable omelet is made by spreading hot thickened creamed vegetables over the omelet just before serving. Asparagus omelet is excellent. Fruit omelets are made by spreading with stewed fruit or jelly or crushed sweetened fresh fruit like strawberries, raspberries or peaches, or jams made of these fruits. Fruit omelets are spread with powdered sugar usually. Rice, macaroni or hominy are often seasoned in a favorite way with cheese or gravy and spread on the omelet before serving. Macaroni cooked with tomatoes and cheese makes an excellent omelet filling. Thickened, stewed tomatoes are nice, and mushrooms may be added with green peas to the tomatoes for Spanish omelet. In fact there are a thousand good combinations and there isn't a nicer way to use a small portion of any left over than to use it for an omelet filling if it will harmonize with eggs at all. Four eggs in an omelet combination of this kind will do nicely for a meal for a family of six people.—Contributed.

BREAD OMELET.—Soak one half cup of bread crumbs in one half cup of milk. Separate four eggs, beat separately. Beat bread crumbs into the yolks, add salt and pepper, beat whites till stiff. Add them to yolks stirring with a spoon and pour into a hot spider at once. Cook on top of stove till the bottom is browned then place in the oven till it is cooked through.—Mrs. Creaser.

HAM OR MEAT OMELETS.—Soak one cupful of bread crumbs in one cup of milk; add one cupful of minced cold boiled ham, veal, beef, corned beef, tongue, fish or chicken; season with salt and pepper. Beat two eggs very light, stir in lightly. Turn into a buttered hot frying pan, brown on the bottom well, then run the pan into a hot oven and brown on top. Or they may be fried in deep lard by dipping a spoonful of the mixture into the smoking hot grease.—Contributed.

CODFISH OMELET.—Cook one tablespoon of flour with one of butter, add one half cup hot milk. Add one cup of shredded codfish that has been parboiled until tender, and drained. Add two cups cold boiled potatoes that have been chopped fine. Mix well. Brown butter in a hot frying pan, turn in the mixture, brown on the bottom, then fold over and serve.—Contributed.

BAKED EGGS.—Break eight eggs into a well buttered dish; salt and pepper them, add bits of butter and four tablespoons of cream; cover top with grated cheese. Bake about twenty minutes.—Contributed.

EGGS WITH MUSHROOMS ON TOAST.—Break one cupful of mushrooms into small pieces, dredge them with flour and put them into the saucepan with three tablespoonfuls of butter, a few drops of onion juice, salt and paprika. Cook for ten minutes. Beat three eggs slightly, not separating them, and season them with salt and pepper. Add them to the mushrooms and scrape them from the bottom as they cook until the mixture is thick and creamy. Serve on hot buttered toast.

Left Overs

"Beware of little extravagances; a small leak will sink a big ship."—Benjamin Franklin.

Left Overs Roll Call Responses

BREAD AND POTATOES.—Break up scraps of bread into small pieces, moisten with a little hot water; cover and steam a few moments. Add to diced cold boiled potatoes, season, and fry in butter.—Mrs. A. McKay.

HASH.—Use twice as much cold boiled potatoes as you have cold cooked meat. Chop fine, separately; mix until moist with hot water and season with salt and cayenne pepper and a little onion, if liked. Spread on baking pan, pour bacon drippings on top and bake brown.—Mrs. T. A. McKay.

EIER BROD.—Cut scraps of bread into small dice and fry brown in plenty of butter. To a pint of crumbs, beat five or six eggs lightly with two or three tablespoons of milk; add a dash of salt and turn eggs over the bread. Scramble all together until the eggs are cooked. Serve hot.—Mrs. Paul Leonhardy.

BROILED BOILED HAM.—Take thin slices of boiled ham, put on a broiler and broil crisp. Nice for breakfast or lunch.—L. W.

SWEET AND SOUR STEW.—Cut up two onions and fry until glazed; add one tablespoon of flour. Brown and add one quart cold water, one bay leaf, a little salt and pepper, one cooking spoon of vinegar and the same of sugar.

add salt and pepper, beat whites till stiff. Add them to yolks stirring with a spoon and pour into a hot spider at once. Cook on top of stove till the bottom is browned then place in the oven till it is cooked through.—Mrs. Creaser.

HAM OR MEAT OMELETS.—Soak one cupful of bread crumbs in one cup of milk; add one cupful of minced cold boiled ham, veal, beef, corned beef, tongue, fish or chicken; season with salt and pepper. Beat two eggs very light, stir in lightly. Turn into a buttered hot frying pan, brown on the bottom well, then run the pan into a hot oven and brown on top. Or they may be fried in deep lard by dipping a spoonful of the mixture into the smoking hot grease.—Contributed.

CODFISH OMELET.—Cook one tablespoon of flour with one of butter, add one half cup hot milk. Add one cup of shredded codfish that has been parboiled until tender, and drained. Add two cups cold boiled potatoes that have been chopped fine. Mix well. Brown butter in a hot frying pan, turn in the mixture, brown on the bottom, then fold over and serve.—Contributed.

BAKED EGGS.—Break eight eggs into a well buttered dish; salt and pepper them, add bits of butter and four tablespoons of cream; cover top with grated cheese. Bake about twenty minutes.—Contributed.

EGGS WITH MUSHROOMS ON TOAST.—Break one cupful of mushrooms into small pieces, dredge them with flour and put them into the saucepan with three tablespoonfuls of butter, a few drops of onion juice, salt and paprika. Cook for ten minutes. Beat three eggs slightly, not separating them, and season them with salt and pepper. Add them to the mushrooms and scrape them from the bottom as they cook until the mixture is thick and creamy. Serve on hot buttered toast.

Left Overs

"Beware of little extravagances; a small leak will sink a big ship."—Benjamin Franklin.

Left Overs Roll Call Responses

BREAD AND POTATOES.—Break up scraps of bread into small pieces, moisten with a little hot water; cover and steam a few moments. Add to diced cold boiled potatoes, season, and fry in butter.—Mrs. A. McKay.

HASH.—Use twice as much cold boiled potatoes as you have cold cooked meat. Chop fine, separately; mix until moist with hot water and season with salt and cayenne pepper and a little onion, if liked. Spread on baking pan, pour bacon drippings on top and bake brown.—Mrs. T. A. McKay.

EIER BROD.—Cut scraps of bread into small dice and fry brown in plenty of butter. To a pint of crumbs, beat five or six eggs lightly with two or three tablespoons of milk; add a dash of salt and turn eggs over the bread. Scramble all together until the eggs are cooked. Serve hot.—Mrs. Paul Leonhardy.

BROILED BOILED HAM.—Take thin slices of boiled ham, put on a broiler and broil crisp. Nice for breakfast or lunch.—L. W.

SWEET AND SOUR STEW.—Cut up two onions and fry until glazed; add one tablespoon of flour. Brown and add one quart cold water, one bay leaf, a little salt and pepper, one cooking spoon of vinegar and the same of sugar.

amcontent.com/pod-product-compliance
Source LLC
rg PA
19100526
0021B/3511